Welcome

Today, she's the name on seemingly everyone's lips, the superstar who has successfully captivated the world with her music, artistry and celebrity status, but how well do you actually know Taylor Swift? Inside, we will explore Taylor's life and career, from her upbringing to her Nashville ambitions and unstoppable climb to music royalty. But that's not all: at the end of each section we will put your Taylor knowledge to the test. Be sure to keep track of your answers because, at the end, we will reveal how true a dedicated Swiftie you are!

In each article you'll find three questions with a range of difficulties – the harder the question, the more points it's worth (Bronze = 1, Silver = 2, Gold = 3) – and a maximum of six points available per article. You'll find the answers in the text, so be sure to pay attention as you read!

So grab a notepad and see how well you know Taylor, then compare scores with friends to discover who's the ultimate superfan! Answers on page 122.

Good luck!

" My parents were very strict about education and hard work, from the time my brother and I were really little kids"

Early life

THE ORIGINS OF THE WORLD'S BIGGEST POP STAR

Taylor Alison Swift was born on 13 December 1989, placing her squarely among the first cohort of millennials in West Reading, Pennsylvania. Her parents, who named their little girl after the singer-songwriter James Taylor, were Scott and Andrea Swift, and she has a younger brother, Austin, who was born in 1992. An attractive part of Swift lore is that she grew up on a Christmas tree farm, which might sound too pleasant to be true – but it's accurate.

"It was such a weird place to grow up," she admitted to *Esquire* in 2014. "But it has cemented in me this unnatural level of excitement about fall and then the holiday season. My friends are so sick of me talking about autumn coming. They're like, 'What are you, an elf?'"

Humble beginnings: Taylor, from the nearby town of Wyomissing, sings the national anthem on 5 April 2007, before the Reading Phillies' opening game against the Harrisburg Senators.

She also recalled that her family all had jobs around the farm, with her allotted task being to "pick the praying mantis pods off of the trees, collecting them so that the bugs wouldn't hatch inside people's houses" – and yes, that does sound a bit icky. "The only reason that was my job was because I was too little to help lift trees," she continued, adding: "My parents were very strict about education and hard work, from the time my brother and I were really little kids."

Taylor first went to preschool and kindergarten at Alvernia Montessori School, a facility run by Franciscan nuns, in line with her Christian upbringing. Later, she attended junior and senior high schools in Wyomissing, Pennsylvania, but she spent her summers in Stone Harbor, New Jersey.

So, was the future pop phenomenon happy at school? Not entirely, she recalls. Hers was a life of privilege (read more from page ten), and Wyomissing was a place where you needed to toe the line: "It mattered what kind of designer handbag you brought to school," she told the writer Lizzie Widdicombe. You've seen the movie *Mean Girls, right*? A lot of that film happened in real life, we're told. "I never felt like the kids in school were right about me when they'd say, 'She's weird. She's annoying. I don't want to hang out with her,'" she told *Esquire*.

Fortunately, Taylor had a higher goal than trying to fit in at school. Even as a little kid, she preferred watching music documentaries on MTV and VH1 to The Disney Channel. She began singing and acting in musical theatre, appearing in youth productions in and out of school, and not long afterwards, Taylor started to write songs and perform at a coffee shop in Stone Harbor.

"I always remember writing in my journal, saying, I just have to keep writing songs. I just have to keep doing this and someday, maybe, this will be different for me. I just have to keep working." To prove that she was serious, she fast-tracked through two years of high school in a single year. "That was just the most practical way to do it," she shrugged. An early sign of the work ethic that has taken her to the very top, we are sure you will agree.

At age 11, Taylor and her mother travelled to Nashville to deliver tapes of the aspiring superstar covering Dolly Parton and The Chicks.

Early life

Taylor (second row, second from left, wearing red) as a youngster at Alvernia Montessori School.

The childhood home of Taylor Swift on Grandview Boulevard in Wyomissing, Pennsylvania; it is shown here shortly after it was sold in 2013.

"I remember writing in my journal, saying, I just have to keep writing songs. I just have to keep doing this and someday, maybe, this will be different for me"

Test your Taylor knowledge!
CAN YOU HIT THE GOLDEN NOTE?

Q1: Who is Taylor named after?

Q2: Name the pesky insects that Taylor removed as part of her farm work.

Q3: Where did Taylor have her first experience of education?

Grab a notepad and pen and see how well you know Taylor.
Answers on p122

Family ties

GET TO KNOW TAYLOR'S PARENTS, BROTHER AND HER FAMOUS GRANDMOTHER!

Taylor's parents Andrea and Scott arrive for a taping of *The Late Show With David Letterman* at in 2014 in New York City.

Family ties

Taylor Swift and her younger brother, Austin, at a 2009 event in Nashville, Tennessee. Austin is now an actor and film producer.

Few musicians make it far without the support of a loyal family, and while that family doesn't have to be wealthy to help their kids make it, a bit of cash in the bank certainly helps. Taylor Swift's father, Scott, and mother, Andrea, who married in 1988, had both worked in the finance industries, the former a stockbroker for Merrill Lynch and the latter a mutual fund marketing executive: the Christmas tree farm on which the family lived was bought from one of Scott's former clients. Scott himself was a formidable name in the money world, said *The New Yorker*, which described him as "a descendant of three generations of bank presidents".

Privilege isn't just about money, though – it's about the cultural depth of one's environment and the value applied to education and hard work. Taylor and her brother Austin were encouraged to work diligently at school – hence the fast-track route that the older Swift took through high school, and – as we've mentioned – the whole family worked on the farm.

Music was a part of Taylor's background, as her maternal grandmother Marjorie Finlay (1928-2003) had been an opera singer. Marjorie, who had enjoyed fame in the 1950s and had even hosted her own TV show in Puerto Rico, was a massive motivator for Taylor.

"She would sing in whatever city-opera production when my grandfather was working: he was an engineer, and he would travel a lot,

11

building bridges," she informed *Esquire*. "She was even a cohost on this show called *The Pan American Show* in Puerto Rico, and she was beautiful and graceful but spoke the worst Spanish you've ever heard. All the Spanish-speaking fans in Puerto Rico just loved her because she was so brave about how terrible she was at speaking Spanish. She tried every night. And then she'd get up and sing, and, of course, it was the perfect, beautiful operatic voice. Gorgeous soprano."

This background, combined with the Swift family's keenness to put in long hours of work

> "The Spanish-speaking fans just loved [my grandmother] because she was so brave about how terrible she was at speaking Spanish"

A young, 17-year-old Taylor Swift at Belmont University in Nashville, Tennessee, way back in 2006.

Taylor, her mother, Andrea, Nicole Kidman and Keith Urban talk in the audience at the Country Music Awards in Las Vegas in April 2010.

Family ties

when necessary ("My dad would get up four hours early to go mow the fields on his tractor," Taylor remembered), made it almost inevitable that when she wanted to become a musician, she wasn't half-hearted about it. This was where Andrea Swift stepped up to help, driving her daughter to karaoke competitions in the late 1990s at weekends, and in 2001 taking her all the way to the famous country music hotspot Nashville, Tennessee, an 800-mile trip from Wyomissing. The object of the trip was to "drop off her karaoke demo tapes around Music Row, in search of a record deal; they didn't succeed, but the experience convinced [Taylor] Swift that she needed a way to stand out," wrote the *New Yorker*.

In later life, Austin Swift has become an actor and producer, while Scott continues to work at Merrill Lynch; both parents help out in various ways with Taylor's career. Both have come through serious illness, with Andrea suffering breast and brain cancer in 2015 and 2019: Taylor wrote 'The Best Day' and 'Soon You'll Get Better' in her mother's honour. At 71 and 65, Scott and Andrea will hopefully enjoy many more years of their daughter's unique achievements.

Test your Taylor knowledge!
CAN YOU HIT THE GOLDEN NOTE?

Q1: Name Taylor's grandmother.

Q2: Where does Scott Swift work?

Q3: Why did the Swifts visit Nashville in 2001?

Grab a notepad and pen and see how well you know Taylor.
Answers on p122

The music that inspired Taylor

WHICH SONGS AND MUSICIANS PROMPTED MS SWIFT TO FOLLOW HER MUSE?

Like many American kids who listened to pop music in the 1990s and 2000s, Taylor Swift was bowled over by the music of Shania Twain, the Canadian singer-songwriter who peaked commercially between 1995 and 2003, although she released a whole lot of music before and after those dates too. You'll know the titles of Twain's signature songs 'You're Still The One', 'That Don't Impress Me Much' and 'Man! I Feel Like A Woman' because they became embedded in the cultural fabric of Western pop culture, thanks to their state-of-the-art production, earworm melodies and mastery of a range of tones, from lovelorn balladry to sly humour at the expense of insecure males everywhere.

Taylor was a teenager for most of Twain's imperial period and placed perfectly for those songs – which, as she told the *Guardian*, "could make you want to just run around the block four times and daydream about everything" – to make maximum impact on her as a budding artist. It's not going too far to state that Twain's work was largely responsible for Taylor's decision to try to enter the field of country music herself, although this wide-eyed kid was also a fan of other country music acts such as The Dixie Chicks (later renamed The Chicks)

The music that inspired Taylor

The great country superstar Dolly Parton performing at the Glastonbury Festival in the UK in 2014.

Eminem, the biggest rapper in the world through the 1990s. A fan upload of Taylor covering 'Lose Yourself' has over 10 million views on YouTube!

Taylor has covered Nicki Minaj's songs on tour, and fans speculate that they could collab officially in the future.

and formidable singers such as Dolly Parton.

This was the background that inspired Taylor to persuade her mother, Andrea, to take her to Nashville, the famous home of country and western, the new country-pop pioneered by Shania Twain and others, and increasing numbers of other musical genres. "Everyone in that town wanted to do what I wanted to do" Taylor later reflected when asked about this initial foray's lack of success. "So, I kept thinking to myself, I need to figure out a way to be different."

Although the Nashville experience didn't lead to a record deal – or much other than a sense of rejection – Taylor wasn't put off by the experience. If anything, the city gave her renewed professionalism, she recalled in subsequent years.

"You hear stories about these artists who show up four hours late to a photoshoot, and in Nashville, that doesn't happen. In Nashville, if you go four hours late to a photoshoot, everyone leaves," she told *Esquire*. "In Nashville, if you don't care about radio and being kind to the people who are being good to you… then they won't take care of you. I've never been more proud to have come from a community that's so rooted in songwriting, so rooted in hard work and in treating people well. It was the best kind of training."

Despite the above influences, Taylor doesn't restrict her tastes to country music. She has often referred to her love of hip-hop music, covering Eminem and Nicki Minaj songs live and saying, "One of the things people don't really recognise about the similarities between country and hip-hop is that they're celebrations of pride in a lifestyle."

Taylor has also expressed her admiration for Joni Mitchell, and once bore a handwritten Bruce Springsteen lyric on her arm for a show: this read, "We learned more from a three-minute record than we ever learned in school" – and who doesn't sympathise with that sentiment?

The Canadian singer Shania Twain was a massive musical influence to a young Taylor Swift in the mid 1990s.

The music that inspired Taylor

Test your Taylor knowledge!
CAN YOU HIT THE GOLDEN NOTE?

🎵 **Q1:** Which country is Shania Twain from?

🎵 **Q2:** What were The Chicks previously called?

🎵 **Q3:** Which hip-hop artists has Taylor covered live?

Grab a notepad and pen and see how well you know Taylor.
Answers on p122

ALBUM Taylor Swift (2006)

HOW ALBUM NUMBER ONE CAME TO LIFE

What's most notable about Taylor Swift's early years as a musician is how quickly she progressed. After the Nashville trip in 2001, she learned the guitar and started writing songs with the help of a computer repairman, who had worked on the Swift family's computer. In 2003, she performed the American national anthem at the US Open tennis tournament in New York, where a manager called Dan Dymtrow approached her: he quickly signed Taylor – still only 14 years old – to the RCA label in Nashville for an artist development deal.

The following year, Scott Swift transferred his job and his family to Nashville to make it easier for Taylor to work there: once ensconced in Tennessee, Taylor assembled an album's worth of songs with a songwriter called Liz Rose – although Rose herself described her role as more of an editor. The RCA contract expired after a year, but a Dreamworks executive, Scott Borchetta, spotted Taylor at a showcase and signed her to his new label, Big Machine Records. This led to the recording of Taylor's self-titled album in 2005 and its release on 24 October the following year.

So what kind of album did we get from Taylor, now 17? She no doubt has her own views about

Album: Taylor Swift

Taylor's first manager Dan Dymtrow (left) and music-industry colleague Michael Brooks pictured at Geisha House in Hollywood.

The great singer-songwriter Tim McGraw: an inspiration to Taylor Swift and many other fans of country music.

Pop luminary Miley Cyrus, Taylor, Guns N' Roses guitarist Slash and Big Machine label owner Scott Borchetta at the 2009 Grammy Salute To Industry Icons in Beverly Hills.

Test your Taylor knowledge!
CAN YOU HIT THE GOLDEN NOTE?

Q1: Who produced Taylor's debut album?

Q2: Who is Tim McGraw?

Q3: How many times did the album *Taylor Swift* (2006) go platinum?

Grab a notepad and pen and see how well you know Taylor.
Answers on p122

Album: Taylor Swift

it all these years later, but there's promise in the songs, written with winning honesty and loaded with catchy hooks. She's credited as a writer on all 11 songs, three as the sole writer, and the album is given a professional sheen by producer Nathan Chapman, with whom Taylor had previously worked on demo recordings.

Most of the songs deal with the themes you would expect from a small-town teenager: romance, musical idols and school experiences among them. The first song and single, 'Tim McGraw', espouses Taylor's hope that a high-school ex-boyfriend will think of her when he hears songs by the eponymous singer. Another, 'Our Song', had already been heard when she played it at a school talent show and deals with another ex with whom she "didn't have a song. So I went ahead and wrote us one". 'Teardrops On My Guitar' is a self-explanatory tale of lost love, while 'Picture To Burn' and 'Should've Said No' are more vengeful in nature, addressing unrequited love. Indeed, 'Cold As You' is the sad epilogue to an entirely loveless relationship.

The 'Tim McGraw' single made number six on the Hot Country Songs chart and number 40 on the *Billboard* 100, while the album itself made number 19 on the latter list. Despite these promising results, it took a while to make an impact, only doing so after a year, by which point it had sold an unexpected million copies. This was attributed partly to Taylor's diligent presence on Myspace, the now long-gone music-focused social media platform, and also to the live dates she performed with country musicians such as Rascal Flatts, George Strait, Brad Paisley – and even Tim McGraw, on whose joint tour with Faith Hill Taylor guested in 2007.

Now, of course, the album is regarded as a triumph, having spent almost 300 weeks on the *Billboard* Top 200 and sold six million copies. You couldn't make its seven-times-platinum story up if you tried…

Producer Nathan Chapman with Taylor backstage at the 2009 Academy Of Country Music Awards in Las Vegas.

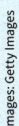

"A six-month headlining tour, Taylor's first, saw her spreading her message across America into the autumn of 2009"

Album: Fearless

Fearless (2008)

WHERE TAYLOR WAS HEADED WITH HER POWERFUL SOPHOMORE ALBUM

While on the road from 2007 to 2008, Taylor didn't waste any of her newfound momentum: she knew that the pressure would be on her to surpass her debut album the next time she entered the studio, and so she devoted time to songwriting. The new tracks continued to focus on romance, a wise move: while other newly famous musicians switched lyrical tack and failed as a result, Taylor knew what her fans wanted to hear. Songwriting partners included Liz Rose once again, as well as the musicians John Rich and Colbie Caillat: with their help, Taylor reportedly came up with as many as 75 new songs.

The final 13 songs that appeared on her second album, *Fearless*, were once again produced by Nathan Chapman, with Taylor herself also getting a production credit. Inspirations included fairytales and William Shakespeare's tragedy *Romeo And Juliet*, with the songs 'Love Story', 'White Horse' and 'Forever & Always' making those sources clear. Then there's 'You Belong With Me', a tale of unachievable romance, and 'The Best Day', the story of a comforting shopping day with her mother Andrea.

Musically, *Fearless* is more pop than country, with *The Guardian* remarking that its only country elements are the song's references to God and one-horse towns. Taylor swerved this debate neatly, reasoning: "[Whether] you tell stories about how you live on a farm and cherish your family and God, or whether you tell stories about being in high school and

All that glitters: Taylor performing at the 2008 Stagecoach Music Festival.

23

Foo Fighters frontman Dave Grohl congratulates Taylor on her nomination onstage during the 2007 Grammys.

Taylor with Joe Jonas, of Jonas Brothers fame – despite her fame and success in the music business, she managed to stay true to herself.

Test your Taylor knowledge!
CAN YOU HIT THE GOLDEN NOTE?

 Q1: What famous play inspired 'Love Story'?

 Q2: Which rock band sang one of Taylor's songs on TV?

 Q3: Which film series was Taylor Lautner famous for?

Grab a notepad and pen and see how well you know Taylor.
Answers on p122

Taylor's personal style started to evolve as she grew more confident with her public persona.

Album: Fearless

being cheated on, they're stories about your life. That's what makes me a country artist."

The album's release on 11 November 2008 was attended by huge publicity, with Taylor invited to perform on a whole host of top TV shows that year and in 2009, including *The Ellen DeGeneres Show*, *Good Morning America*, *Late Night With David Letterman*, *Saturday Night Live* and a special episode of *CMT Crossroads* on which she and the pop-metal band Def Leppard sang each other's songs. Multiple high-profile awards ceremonies followed, including the Country Music Association Awards, the American Music Awards, the 51st Grammy Awards and an infamous slot at the MTV Video Music Awards, which you can read about shortly.

A six-month headlining tour, Taylor's first, saw her spreading the message across America into the autumn of 2009; the following year, extra dates took her to Australia and Japan, grossing over $63 million – perhaps a sign of things to come?

By now Taylor Swift was a bona fide star. At just 21 years old in 2010, she was the hottest new musical act to emerge in years: some journalists were predicting that she would be the biggest-selling new female artist since Madonna. All credit to Taylor: she kept her head despite her giddying rise to fame, and made a decent attempt to enter the world of acting with a film, *Valentine's Day*, and an episode of *CSI*. Even when tabloid attention maxed out once she'd acquired a celebrity boyfriend, *Twilight*'s brooding werewolf Taylor Lautner, she stayed calm, focused and serene. Could any of us have done the same?

> ❝ At just 21 years old, Taylor was the hottest new musical act to emerge in years: some journalists were predicting that she would be the biggest-selling new female artist since Madonna ❞

25

You need to calm down!

THE MOMENTS THAT HIT THE HEADLINES AND BLEW OUR MINDS

The road to fame and fortune is paved with lawsuits, and over the years, Taylor Swift has regularly been a target of controversy. A typical example of the cases Taylor gets pulled into is from 2017, where the songwriters behind 3LW's 2001 single 'Playas Gon' Play' sued her thanks to the similarity of lines in the song 'Shake It Off'. Taylor replied, "Until learning about [the] plaintiffs' claim in 2017, I had never heard the song 'Playas Gon' Play' and had never heard of that song or the group 3LW." The suit was dropped at the end of 2022.

Perhaps a more legitimate criticism of Taylor is the issue of owning a private jet and its concomitant CO_2 emissions. When a marketing firm named Taylor as the number-one problem in this field, her rep responded, "Taylor's jet is loaned out regularly to other individuals. To attribute most or all of these trips to her is blatantly incorrect." However, criticism was renewed when we learned she continues to use

People often get the wrong end of the stick: is Taylor and her former boyfriend Harry Styles having a heated exchange here? Here, it's a little unclear, but another picture from the same event shows them bumping fists, showing they're obviously pals.

You need to calm down!

The infamous moment Kanye West invaded the 2009 VMA stage to shame Taylor while she was accepting the Best Female Video award.

her jet to dart during touring breaks to support her boyfriend, Travis Kelce, in Kansas City.

Taylor attracted criticism in her earlier years for keeping her politics private, although she is more vocal nowadays. However, as she explained, the fate of The Chicks – who had been attacked by the right wing in 2003 after criticising the then-President George W Bush – had led her to keep quiet. "It terrified me," she said. "These days, with social media, people can be so mad about something one day and then forget what they were mad about a couple weeks later. That's fake outrage. But what happened to [The Chicks] was real outrage… you're always one comment away from being done being able to make music."

Feuds are always the target of speculation, and the story of Taylor Swift and Katy Perry is notorious, with the two throwing insults at each other for what seemed like forever: the former called the latter her 'straight-up enemy'. This story has a happy ending with the two burying the hatchet and Perry appearing in the video for 'You Need To Calm Down'.

We can't *not* mention the infamous time Taylor fell out with the rapper Kanye West in 2009 when he ran on stage during her acceptance speech at that year's VMA ceremony. Grabbing the mic from her, the musician went into an unhinged rant about how Beyoncé Knowles should have won the award, leaving Taylor literally speechless. Kanye's actions then and afterwards were reprehensible and have been emblematic of the problematic singer's decline.

West's then-wife Kim Kardashian got involved, which spun off into a splinter feud. The upshot is that Taylor was able to use this time in her life to her advantage, using elements of this battle – among other things – as inspiration for her defiant *Reputation* album. Talk about making lemonade out of lemons…

Damon Albarn from the band Blur slandered Taylor out of the blue, accusing her of not writing her songs. Taylor, rightfully so, clapped back in classy fashion on Twitter.

Test your Taylor knowledge!
CAN YOU HIT THE GOLDEN NOTE?

Q1: What is the name of 3LW's song?

Q2: Why is Taylor using her private jet?

Q3: Who did Taylor call a 'straight-up enemy'?

Grab a notepad and pen and see how well you know Taylor.
Answers on p122

You need to calm down!

Taylor and Katy Perry started out as friends but then began a fiery feud, however, the two are now on good terms.

Taylor has recently come under fire for using her private jet to visit her boyfriend Travis Kelce.

Music evolution

HOW HAS TAYLOR CHANGED HER MUSICAL APPROACH OVER THE YEARS?

As you read this, it's been almost 20 years since Taylor Swift released her first album – a lifetime in the pop music world, you'll agree, given that stars come and stars go with alarming frequency. This is not the case, broadly speaking, in the more conservative world of country music, where audiences are generally loyal for longer and where musical trends hold no sway because the nature and themes of the songs themselves evolve slowly, if at all.

Does Taylor fit into either of these two worlds more than the other? Not unless you're a purist. The reality is she hasn't made purely country music since her first couple of albums, and even then, her songs always benefited from a pop-friendly production. As *Rolling Stone* once wrote, "When The Dixie Chicks bashed Bush and fell from Nashville grace in 2003, a huge space opened up in the heart of the country audience... Taylor Swift has completely filled it, adding a little something for their soccer daughters with a sound that's not just rock-informed but teen-poppy too."

By 2012 and the *Red* album, Taylor had moved on from that sound, introducing elements of rock and dance music into her sound, leading

Music evolution

While Taylor's musical style changed over time, she was never far from a guitar or piano on-stage.

By the 1989 album, Taylor had morphed into a pop musician, often performing dance routines on stage like this one from November 2015.

some critics to accuse her of betraying her roots. One writer, Jody Rosen, stated that she had made a "bait-and-switch manoeuvre, planting roots in loamy country soil, then pivoting to pop", which was a slightly harsh but also accurate observation.

With that understood, elements of her roots – country instrumentation and a storytelling approach – have lingered long in her albums. You can take the girl out of the country, but you can't take the country completely out of the girl, it seems – and in any case, her musical evolution has met with both critical and commercial approval.

"You can take the girl out of the country, but you can't take the country completely out of the girl, it seems"

Taylor pictured in 2016: could there be a more different look than the long ringlets and cowboy boots of a decade before?

As Taylor's success grew, she became more confident with experimenting. With *Reputation*, she added R&B into the mix.

Music evolution

"Taylor Swift is a musical chameleon," wrote the BBC in 2022. "[She] generally changes lanes every two albums... Over the course of 16 years and nine albums, she's switched genres from country to pop to alternative to folk." Of the *Reputation* album, *Now Toronto* concluded that it was "a final and complete rejection of her pop-country roots, incorporating dubstep, R&B and harder-edged styles of EDM into the mix." NPR added, "Swift has relocated herself far from country music on her new album... this one is her move into electronic dance music."

These writers knew what they were talking about, and when *Lover* (2019) went into hip-hop and trap, *Folklore* and *Evermore* (2020) boasted folk and indie styles and *Midnights* (2022) offered us experimental pop, they were proven right once again. Taylor is not the first musician to do this – The Beatles, David Bowie and Madonna all shed several skins across their careers – but she is the first, and perhaps the last, to do so with such consistent success and longevity in the new millennium.

Think about what this means: Taylor Swift is an artist like no other. Her grasp of style, depth of perception and vision over time is unparalleled in 2024 – whether as a country artist, a pop singer, or any other genre you care to mention.

Test your Taylor knowledge!
CAN YOU HIT THE GOLDEN NOTE?

Q1: Which one of Taylor's inspirations 'bashed Bush'?

Q2: Which Taylor Swift album first incorporated dubstep?

Q3: Which three artists did we mention that often changed their styles, like Taylor?

Grab a notepad and pen and see how well you know Taylor.
Answers on p122

> "Red debuted at the top of the Billboard 200 chart, becoming the fastest-selling country album ever"

People began to notice the formidable Taylor Swift media machine when she showed up time and again to relentlessly promote *Red*.

Switching colours for a moment: Taylor at the Elie Saab Spring/Summer 2013 show as part of Paris Fashion Week.

Taylor's calling card for this era was an ever-present red shade of lipstick, and maybe a hat if she was feeling fancy.

Album: Red

ALBUM Red (2012)

A CLASSIC TAYLOR ERA UNDER THE MICROSCOPE

By 2011, *Speak Now* had set new sales records worldwide, but its creator – and sole songwriter – wasn't going to sit around and count her laurels. By the autumn of that year, Taylor Swift had 25 new songs ready to go, with the plan this time around to expand and diversify her sound using a range of producers. This was a concept that came with a certain degree of risk, of course, but this was exactly the time to start taking those risks.

So what did album four, *Red*, sound like on its release on 22 October 2012? Well, for the first time, a synth-heavy, electronic pop sound was at front and centre thanks to the recruitment of the Swedish producers Max Martin and Shellback – see '22', 'I Knew You Were Trouble', and the huge hit 'We Are Never Ever Getting Back Together' for evidence. There's still country-flavoured music here, wisely, with

Test your Taylor knowledge!
CAN YOU HIT THE GOLDEN NOTE?

Q1: Which singers duetted with Taylor on *Red*?

Q2: Which songs did Max Martin produce?

Q3: Which seven songs from *Red* appeared as singles?

Grab a notepad and pen and see how well you know Taylor.
Answers on p122

Album: Red

Taylor and pop powerhouse Ed Sheeran sang 'Everything Has Changed' together on *Red*.

'Stay Stay Stay' and 'Sad Beautiful Tragic' reassuring the fans that Taylor hadn't abandoned her core sound completely, and there's stadium-sized rock with 'Everything Has Changed' and 'The Last Time', duets with Ed Sheeran and Snow Patrol singer Gary Lightbody respectively.

Add it all up, and the result is that *Red* is a country-tinged pop album – an easy description to land on from today's point of view. Back in 2012, the new direction caused the debate to rage. *Rolling Stone* called it "post-country rock"; *The LA Times* labelled it "perfectly rendered American popular music"; and *American Songwriter* stated that it was "iPod shuffle-fluidly", which makes a kind of sense. Lyrically, Taylor discussed 'red' emotions such as "intense love, intense frustration, jealousy, confusion" and hinted at sexual attraction for the first time, a fact noted by more than a few critics.

Red and its seven singles – 'We Are Never Ever Getting Back Together', 'Begin Again', 'Red', 'I Knew You Were Trouble', 'State of Grace', 'Everything Has Changed' and the UK-only 'The Last Time' – did as expected, dominating the world's music charts all over again. The gamble of 'going pop' had paid off, although some of Taylor's older, country-devoted fans might have griped a little. The album debuted at the top of the *Billboard* 200 chart with first-week sales of 1,208,000 copies, becoming the fastest-selling country album ever, despite its new direction: it eventually went seven times platinum, a genuinely astounding achievement.

To say that Taylor did a lot of press for the album, or to observe that she played a major tour in its wake, is to understate what happened next. She talked to more than 70 radio stations worldwide, she appeared on *Good Morning America*, *Ellen*, *20/20*, the MTV Video Music Awards, the Country Music Association Awards and the American Music Awards.

As for the arenas-and-stadiums *Red* Tour that ran through 2013 and the first half of 2014, it included 11 sold-out shows at LA's Staples Center, breaking a record; a sold-out show at Sydney Football Stadium that made her the first female artist to do so; and the fastest ticket sales in history in Shanghai. Taylor's dominance was now truly global: it seemed that embracing pop music had paid off.

Taylor rocking New Year's Eve 2013 at Times Square in New York City.

ALBUM
1989
(2014)

RECORDING HER FIFTH ALBUM AND TAKING A STAND

"I leave the genre labelling to other people," Taylor Swift told *The Wall Street Journal* in 2015, a genius bit of marketing that both exempted her from commentary about her new musical direction post-*Red* and reminded readers how pointless such labelling is. It also freed her up from worrying about where to go next with her music, which was just as well because she had plenty to concern herself with – not least a short-lived and much-chatted-about fling with Harry Styles, then as now the hottest solo male singer in the world.

She also relocated from Nashville to New York, a literal as well as artistic step away from her country roots, and hired a powerhouse publicity manager called Tree Paine to handle the endless attention of the media. Paine, who had cut her teeth managing No Doubt, Snoop Dogg, Nine Inch Nails, Marilyn Manson and other artists at the Interscope label, replaced Taylor's long-time PR Paula Erickson in the new post.

The success of the *Red* album, a country-pop hybrid, obliged Taylor to choose one genre or another for album number five: as she put it, in a brilliantly country-style statement, "If you chase two rabbits, you lose them both." This time she looked at 1980s synth music for inspiration, with artists such as Peter Gabriel and the Eurythmics in mind. Her main collaborators on

Collaborator Jack Antonoff and Taylor perform onstage at the Grammy Awards at Staples Center in February 2016 in Los Angeles.

Album: 1989

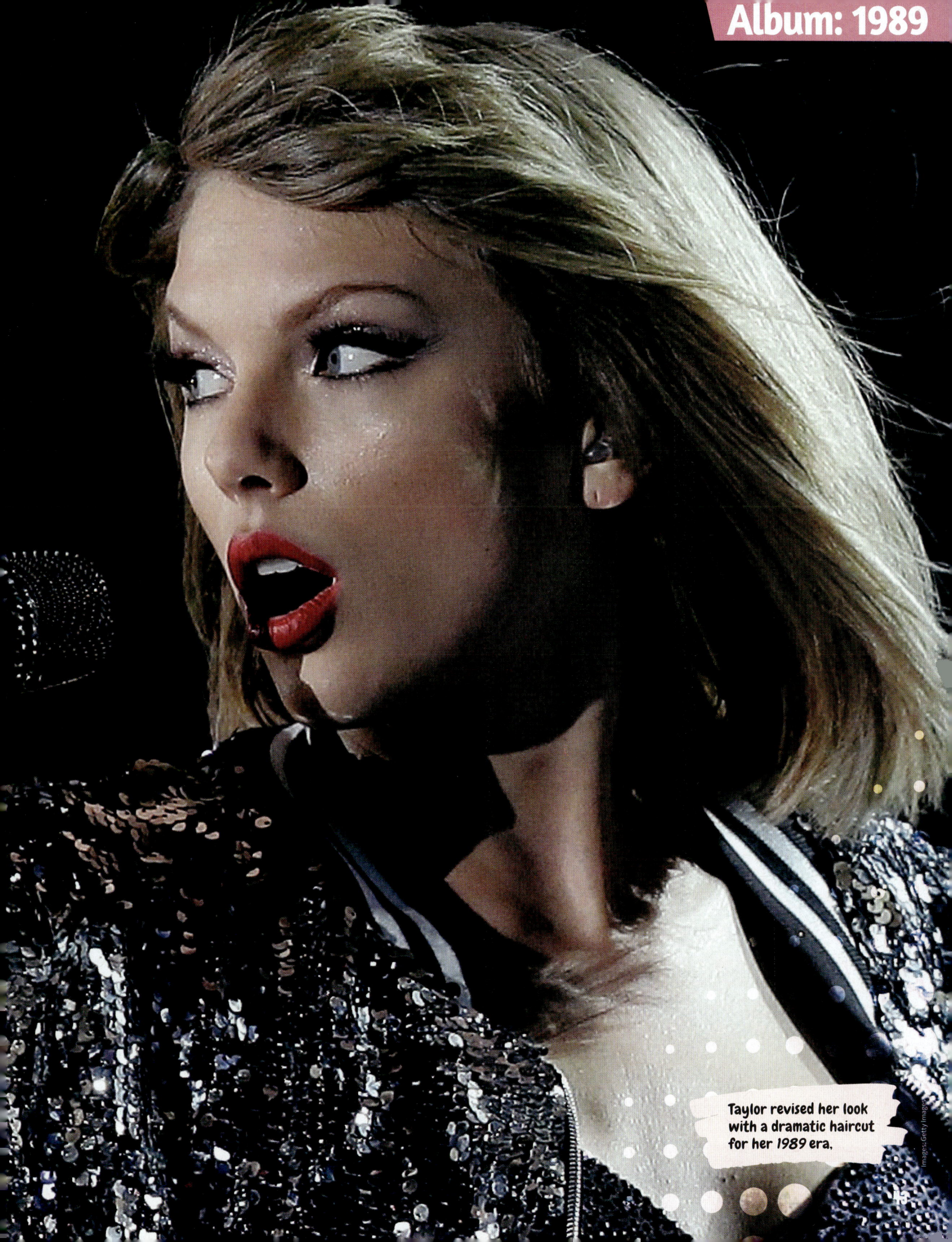

Taylor revised her look with a dramatic haircut for her 1989 era.

the new album, which turned out to be *1989*, were Max Martin and Shellback once again – an obvious choice for the new sounds. Producer Jack Antonoff, with whom Taylor had previously worked, also came on board, as did another producer, Imogen Heap, and Taylor's usual collaborator Nathan Chapman.

The results were both finely-crafted and acclaimed, with the funky 'Style', the hip-hop-influenced 'Blank Space', the indie/synth 'Out Of The Woods' and the amazing dance-pop hit 'Shake It Off' revealing Taylor's effortless mastery of yet more sounds. The beats and poppy keyboards of many of the tracks – 'I Know Places' and 'I Wish You Would' among them – as well as the very 1980s vibe of the self-explanatory 'New Romantics', combine to make Taylor's transition away from country mostly, if not totally, complete.

On 27 October 2014, *1989* was released to similar commercial success and critical acclaim as its immediate predecessors, and a vast, $250 million-grossing world tour ran from May to December 2015, but many Swifties remember this period in their idol's career mostly for a battle in which she engaged in late 2014 with the streaming service Spotify. After writing in *The Wall Street Journal* in the summer that albums as a concept were under threat from streams, she removed her entire catalogue from Spotify that November. A threat to do the same for Apple Music in June 2015 resulted in that service revising its policies: Taylor's music didn't return to Spotify until June 2017.

Such is the power of the Swift brand that, while her worries about music streaming versus album sales have more or less come true, her own work has defeated that tendency. *1989* has gone on to sell over 12 million copies: Taylor Swift had once again came out on top.

> "Taylor looked at 1980s synth music for inspiration, with artists such as Peter Gabriel and the Eurythmics in mind."

Test your Taylor knowledge!
CAN YOU HIT THE GOLDEN NOTE?

Q1: Where did Taylor move from Nashville?

Q2: Name five producers who worked on 1989.

Q3: Name one of Taylor's 1980s inspirations.

Grab a notepad and pen and see how well you know Taylor.
Answers on p122

1989's throwback aesthetic and music proved to be a massive hit with Swifties and the wider public.

Album: 1989

Star-crossed lovers: Taylor Swift and Harry Styles had a brief romance towars the end of 2012.

A sense of style

HOW THE SWIFT LOOK HAS EVOLVED OVER THE ERAS

For half of her almost-35 years on this planet, Taylor Swift has been in the public eye – so that's 17 years of being styled and photographed, with her various looks analysed, critiqued and copied. We would all change our style noticeably over such a long period, but in Taylor's case, with her look an artistic statement as much as her music, she's had more reason to change up her appearance than most people.

Remember how she looked back in 2006? A fresh-faced country kid whose mission was to win everybody's hearts, Taylor appeared with tight blonde ringlets, sundresses and cowboy boots. "I wear cowboy boots so that when I walk down the stairs [at awards ceremonies] I won't fall," she told *Entertainment Weekly* in 2007. By the *Fearless* album, she'd expanded her look with ballgowns, bodices, sequins and even corsets to tie in with the princesses-and-fairytales vibe, swapping out the country boots for heels and riding footwear. When *Speak Now* came along, Taylor began to rock the red lipstick which remains a Swift trademark to this day, and also connected with her long-time stylist Joseph Cassell Falconer for the first time.

The *Red* album saw Taylor upgrade her look significantly, assisted by Falconer. By now she was seen wearing Marina Toybina tops and Bleulab shorts on stage, while in her downtime she slipped into French Connection sweaters

Famous fashionistas gather (left to right): musician Ryan Tedder, Justin Timberlake and Taylor at the 2015 iHeartRadio Music Awards in Los Angeles.

A sense of style

and Theory pants. She also dipped into what she called a '50s housewife' look, with collared shirts paired with high-waisted shorts and pearls. The colour palette was black, white, navy and red, and Taylor's hair was now sleek, with a set of bangs.

For 2014's *1989* album, Taylor acquired garments by Jessica Jones, Alice + Olivia and Atelier Versace among other designers, and wore her hair as a shoulder-grazing bob, perhaps because she was now living in chic New York. Matching crop tops and skirts were often seen, usually accompanied by designer heels. This severe look didn't last too long, though, with Taylor wearing dark-coloured hoodies, combat boots and cargo pants for 2016's *Reputation*, although the edges were smoothed off with Louis Vuitton and Balenciaga garments and snake-logo jewellery.

Where next? To the designers J Mendel, Rosa Bloom, Sophia Webster, Zadig & Voltaire, N:Philanthropy and One Teaspoon for *Lover* in 2019, focusing now on pastels, tie-dyed separates and more sequins for that album's bubblegum pop. A year later, Taylor flipped towards comfortable sweaters, plaid coats, florals and velvets for the pandemic-era *Folklore* and *Evermore* albums, understanding like the rest of us that comfort and security were what we needed at that time.

By 2022 and Taylor's most recent album, *Midnights*, she was wearing Stella McCartney and Roberto Cavalli, harking back to 1970s disco couture with crystals from Oscar de la Renta, corduroy pants and blue eyeshadow. It's a joyous look, and a highlight of The Eras Tour, in which Taylor manages to cram most of the looks mentioned above into a single three-hour performance. Her wardrobe staff must be doing a heck of a lot of overtime.

Rocking the country look back in 2007, when the phrase 'haute couture' hadn't yet entered the Swift narrative.

Test your Taylor knowledge!
CAN YOU HIT THE GOLDEN NOTE?

Q1: For what percentage of her life as Taylor been a celeb?

Q2: Who is her loyal stylist?

Q3: What is a running trend through Taylor's different styles?

Grab a notepad and pen and see how well you know Taylor.
Answers on p122

A sense of style

Taylor towers above designer Gilles Mendel at the Costume Institute Gala in New York City in 2013.

Working hand in hand

WHO HAS TAYLOR COLLABORATED WITH SO FAR?

To her credit, Taylor Swift has always been aware that supporting other musicians and having them assist her, in turn, isn't just a decent thing to do: it's a great way to double exposure and to learn from one's peers. To this end, she has frequently performed with artists who would normally not cross her path, musically speaking, and everyone has benefited from this.

Where do we start? Plenty of the most iconic, fruitful or successful Taylor-plus-everyone-else collabs are coming up, but you can easily dig out more, as the list is almost endless!

In 2008, we heard Taylor in an early assist with the country singer Kellie Pickler on the song 'Best Days Of Your Life'. The same year, singer Colbie Caillat appeared on 'Breathe', taken from Taylor's second album *Fearless*. In 2009, Taylor sang with the rapper T-Pain at that year's CMT Music Awards, performing 'Thug Story', a parody take on her own 'Love Story', and appeared with the pop-rock band Boys Like Girls on their song 'Two Is Better Than One'. That same year, Taylor also sang with John Mayer on his song 'Half Of My Heart'.

Taylor, Zayn and his then-partner Gigi Hadid taking a stroll in New York City around the time the singers worked on the *Fifty Shades Darker* tune 'I Don't Wanna Live Forever'.

Taylor chats with Lana Del Rey at the MTV EMA's in November 2012. The two would later collab ten years later on *Midnights* in 2022.

Working hand in hand

Phoebe Bridgers and Taylor Swift attend the 2023 iHeartRadio Music Awards at Dolby Theatre in Los Angeles on 27 March 2023.

Taylor pictured with frequent collaborators Aaron Dessner (The National) and Jack Antonoff (Fun, Bleachers).

Test your Taylor knowledge!
CAN YOU HIT THE GOLDEN NOTE?

Q1: What did Taylor change the name 'Love Story' to?

Q2: What was Taylor's Scandinavian pen name?

Q3: Who formed Big Red Machine?

Grab a notepad and pen and see how well you know Taylor.
Answers on p122

Working hand in hand

In 2012, Taylor co-wrote and sang on 'Both Of Us' by the rapper B.O.B., addressing racism and bullying in the lyrics, and the following year sang 'Highway Don't Care' alongside Tim McGraw and Keith Urban, a pure country tune that contrasted neatly with Ed Sheeran's slot on 'Everything Has Changed' from her *Red* album.

In 2014, the rapper Kendrick Lamar appeared on a remix of the *1989* single 'Bad Blood'; in 2016, Taylor co-wrote 'This Is What You Came For' by DJ Calvin Harris under the pseudonym Nils Sjöberg; and in 2017, she enjoyed a hit alongside Zayn with 'I Don't Wanna Live Forever' for the soundtrack to the steamy film *Fifty Shades Darker*.

In 2018, Taylor appeared on two songs by the supergroup Big Red Machine, formed by members of The National and Bon Iver, soon-to-be frequent Swift collaborators, and on the song 'Babe' by the country music duo Sugarland. In 2019, we saw Taylor working with Shawn Mendes (on a remix of 'Lover'), Brendon Urie (on 'Me!' from *Lover*) and The Chicks on her song 'Soon You'll Get Better'. In 2020, Haim performed on her song 'No Body, No Crime'. That same year, Bon Iver helped on Taylor's songs 'Evermore' and 'Exile', and The National assisted with 'Coney Island'.

Was she done with collaborations yet? Heck no! Chris Stapleton sang on Taylor's 'I Bet You Think About Me' and Phoebe Bridgers sang on 'Nothing New'. Keith Urban then duetted on 'That's When' from *Fearless (Taylor's Version)*, while Taylor sang on Haim's single 'Gasoline'. The amazing Lana Del Rey guested on the *Midnights* song 'Snow On The Beach', and Hayley Williams performed on 'Castles Crumbling'. Finally, for now, Taylor appeared on The National's 'The Alcott' in 2023 and Fall Out Boy played on her song 'Electric Touch'.

Let's not forget the producer and Bleachers singer Jack Antonoff, a loyal Swift collaborator since 2012. His style perfectly complements her composition methods, and the partnership works both ways. "Taylor's the first person who let me produce a song," he said. "Before Taylor, everyone said: 'You're not a producer'. It took Taylor Swift to say: 'I like the way this sounds'."

> ❝ Taylor has performed with artists who would normally not cross her path ❞

Taylor with the singer Colbie Caillat, the two collaborated on the track 'Breathe' from *Fearless*.

Rapper T-Pain and Taylor at the 2009 CMT Music Awards. The duo performed 'Thug Story' together for the event.

Taylor fully vibing with her music at the piano in Texas in early 2017.

Album: Reputation

ALBUM
Reputation
(2017)

THE MOMENT THAT MADE TAYLOR RETHINK HER APPROACH TO THE MEDIA, TO MUSIC, AND TO HER ENTIRE CAREER

There comes a point when celebrity life becomes too much for anyone, and for Taylor Swift, that moment came around 2016, thanks to a level of cultural dominance that was almost unhealthy. The *1989* album of 2014 had been such a monstrous success that a certain percentage of her audience began to resent her, with her private life and personal and business dealings being scrutinised for flaws. Her feud with Kanye West and Kim Kardashian had divided pop-culture fans into two camps; the press disparaged her brief relationships with Calvin Harris and Tom Hiddleston; and 'pap walks' with her girl squad seemed too good to be true – *The Daily Telegraph* described them as "impossibly beautiful women flaunting impossibly perfect lives". Little wonder, then, that 2017's *Reputation* album was full of emotions, among them bitterness and anger. Taylor described it as a defence mechanism against the media and wrote in-depth for the first time about the pressures of fame and the betrayal. An unlikely inspiration came from the TV series *Game Of Thrones*, she added (spoilers!), the murder of the untrustworthy Littlefinger by the sisters Sansa and Arya Stark triggering 'I Did Something Bad', for example.

Musically, the new album is mostly EDM and R&B, with prominent bass and drums – see '...Ready for It?', 'End Game' – which features Ed Sheeran – 'I Did Something Bad' and 'Don't Blame Me' for examples. The big hit, 'Look What You Made Me Do', combines synths and guitars, but there's softer material too, namely 'Getaway Car', 'Call It What You Want' and the piano-based 'New Year's Day'.

Taylor being photographed on outings with her friends bafflingly became a target of backlash from the media, which directly inspired the music of Reputation.

Touring the world with Reputation

LOOKING BACK AT TAYLOR'S REPUTATION TOUR AND THE HOOK-UP WITH NETFLIX

Taylor Swift's Eras tour, ongoing as we write these words, may well end up being the biggest-grossing live music tour in history – but Taylor's previous run of dates, the record-breaking *Reputation Stadium Tour*, is equally important, both in the affections of Swifties but also because it prepared the ground for the epic Eras tour. Let's see how that huge undertaking came to pass.

In the summer of 2017, Taylor's team announced that tickets would be available for live dates in 2018 via Ticketmaster's Verified Fan programme, a way of stopping bots and ticket scalpers from snapping them up. Presale access was granted to fans who helped to raise awareness of the tour, and the tickets were made available to the rest of the public on Taylor's 28th birthday, 13 December. Notice that the show already had a larger-than-life feel: clearly, this was history in the making.

Making hiss-tory: Taylor performs alongside a scaly friend on 11 May 2018 in Santa Clara, California.

Touring the world with Reputation

As soon as the first dates were announced, ticket demand was so high that extra shows were added to each city. 40 tour dates in North America and five in Oceania were announced, and the show kicked off on 8 May 2018. With Camila Cabello and Charli XCX on board as the opening acts, each concert featured around 19 songs plus 'surprise' cuts that Taylor dropped in between sections of the performance.

Camila and Charli made an appearance mid-set in 'Shake It Off', and every few shows, a special guest arrived to share the mic: these included Shawn Mendes, Troye Sivan, Selena Gomez, Niall Horan, Robbie Williams (on 'Angels', in London), Hayley Kiyoko, Bryan Adams ('Summer Of '69' in Toronto), Tim McGraw and Faith Hill (on, yep, 'Tim McGraw'), Maren Morris and Sugarland.

Make no mistake, it was quite a spectacle. A movable LED screen moved around, both vertically and horizontally; the audience members all wore electronic light bracelets; the stage resembled a futuristic building, with cranes reaching high above the venue; and massive models of snakes appeared on stage, a sly reference to some of the drama of recent times. Taylor herself powered through the songs like an artist possessed, executing constant wardrobe changes and engaging

Holding up nicely: Taylor supported by her backing dancers mid-pose pose.

> ❝ As soon as the dates were announced, ticket demand was so high that extra shows were added to each city ❞

❝ **Rolling Stone called it Taylor's "most astounding tour yet [with] maximum stadium-rock razzle-dazzle bombast"**

Test your Taylor knowledge!

CAN YOU HIT THE GOLDEN NOTE?

Q1: Which two acts opened the shows on the *Reputation* Stadium Tour?

Q2: Which song did Taylor sing with Robbie Williams?

Q3: What platform did Taylor release her tour film on?

Grab a notepad and pen and see how well you know Taylor.
Answers on p122

Touring the world with Reputation

Taylor performs on the opening night of the *Reputation* Stadium Tour at the University of Phoenix Stadium on 8 May 2018 in Glendale, Arizona.

with the massive crowds of fans as if they were old friends.

Fans and the media alike got on board quickly. *Rolling Stone* called it Taylor's "most astounding tour yet [with] maximum stadium-rock razzle-dazzle bombast", and when Taylor walked out on stage into the light, *The Guardian* wrote that it was a "'now I'm here' moment, as Freddie Mercury would once have put it". The numbers revealed the tour's remarkable success, confirming a take of $180 million from 33 dates in North America, with sold-out venues worldwide and new attendance records constantly set.

Fortunately for anyone who missed the shows, Netflix screened a documentary on New Year's Eve 2018, called *Taylor Swift: Reputation Stadium Tour*, produced by Taylor herself and directed by Paul Dugdale. Filmed at the AT&T Stadium in Arlington, Texas on the final date of the US tour leg, the film was a well-crafted close-up of the show, both on and off-stage. See it if you haven't already: it was the last look any of us had of Taylor live for five long years.

Opening act Camila Cabello meets a screaming crowd of Swifties in Arizona: can you imagine the pressure?

High-school buddies Abigail Anderson Berard and Taylor Swift attend the Grammy Awards in LA in February 2015.

New Zealand singer Lorde and Taylor laugh it up at a pre-Grammys gala in 2014.

Squad goals

Taylor and actor/model Cara Delevingne perform a New York pap walk in April 2014.

Squad goals

WHO'S IN TAYLOR'S CREW? LET'S MEET THE GANG...

When the world is watching you, snickering about your every move and seemingly waiting for you to fail, you'd better have people around you that you can rely on. Sure, your family will be there for you when you need them – but do they know about the pressures you face as a famous person, and how to deal with them? No, and nor should they. This is why well-known people tend to connect with other well-known people – and in Taylor Swift's case, there's a whole 'squad' of trusted loved ones for the singer to fall back on.

The original squad from the late 2000s and early 2010s included the singer and actor Selena Gomez, models Martha Hunt and Gigi Hadid, and Taylor's high-school friend Abigail Anderson Berard. Gomez and Taylor had first met as far back as 2005 when they were both dating one of the pop trio, The Jonas Brothers. "She was the girl with the big curly hair and

Fans speculate this iconic pap walk was to show Taylor and Selena Gomez's solidarity with actor Sophie Turner (centre, blue blazer) after she was blindsided by divorce papers and a media attack from her husband Joe Jonas.

Test your Taylor knowledge!
CAN YOU HIT THE GOLDEN NOTE?

Q1: How did Taylor meet Selena Gomez?

Q2: Who is Abigail Anderson Berard?

Q3: What is a 'pap walk'?

Grab a notepad and pen and see how well you know Taylor.
Answers on p122

Squad goals

the bracelets, and the cowboy boots, and I was definitely up-and-coming. We just clicked," Gomez remembered. The two sang together often; notably, Gomez made a surprise vocal appearance on Taylor's *Reputation* tour.

Once Taylor had joined the celebrity A-list, often she was glimpsed at fashion events such as the 2014 Victoria's Secret Fashion Show, where she met Martha Hunt. The two later visited Taylor's childhood home after a show in Pennsylvania and hung out in New York. Gigi Hadid also joined the squad in 2014, describing the group of friends as a source of female empowerment. On the arrival of Hadid's son, fathered by former One Direction singer Zayn, Taylor sent Hadid a handmade blanket. As for Abigail Anderson Berard, this friendship is a rare example of one that survives the runaway fame of one of the participants: they attended the Grammy awards together in 2015, Taylor was Berard's bridesmaid two years later, and the song 'Fifteen' is said to be about Berard.

As the years have passed, Taylor's close friendships have evolved, as they do for all of us. Along the way, the following creative types have claimed squad membership, whether that holds true in the future or not: models Lily Aldridge and Karlie Kloss; actors Lena Dunham, Dianna Agron, Emma Stone, Jaime King, Ruby Rose, Blake Lively, Hailee Steinfeld, Cara Delevingne and Sophie Turner; YouTuber Todrick Hall; singers Ed Sheeran, Ellie Goulding, Camila Cabello and Lorde; jewellery designer Claire Winter Kislinger; and stylist Ashley Avignone.

You will have seen Taylor plus any number of these friends out and about at various locations, and while they're all having a genuinely good time on these so-called 'pap walks' – named after the swarms of paparazzi that doggedly follow them – even the biggest Swiftie will admit that there's something a little pre-planned about these events.

Still, we look at it like this: rather than have press photographers intrude on Taylor's personal life and downtime, she gives them what they want on these pap walks, and then they don't need to bother her elsewhere. That's media management, essentially, and just one more reason why Taylor is a perfect example of the modern, switched-on pop star.

Taylor celebrating her 34th birthday with actor Miles Teller and his wife Keleigh.

ALBUM
Lover (2019)

UP CLOSE AND PERSONAL WITH TAYLOR'S 2019 ERA

After the pop transformation of *1989*, the Kanye West brouhaha and then the darker, defensive *Reputation* album, Taylor Swift needed to redefine her musical direction. And she did that perfectly with the seventh album, *Lover*, released on 23 August 2019. As she told *Vogue*, the new collection was a "love letter to love, in all of its maddening, passionate, exciting, enchanting, horrific, tragic, wonderful glory".

Produced with Jack Antonoff again with other producers such as Joel Little, Sounwave, Frank Dukes and Louis Bell, *Lover* is a lighter album than *Reputation*, using acoustic instruments and piano. As you'd expect, relationships and the relevant emotions are the focal point for this album, with 'I Forgot That You Existed' a kiss-off to a forgotten betrayer, 'I Think He Knows' a confident assertion in a relationship, and 'False God' an examination of fake commitments.

'London Boy' may or may not refer to a certain former boy-band singer (any guesses?), 'Me!' is about self-acceptance, and 'Afterglow' is about taking and accepting blame – and these are

Backstage with Halsey and Jennifer Hudson at the 2019 Billboard Music Awards. Taylor and Jennifer starred in a certain film together, which we'll get to in just a moment...

Album: Lover

Taylor performing at the *Time* 100 Gala in New York, with a Lover-decorated guitar.

67

Performing with Brendon Urie of Panic! At The Disco at the 2019 Billboard Music Awards in Las Vegas.

Test your Taylor knowledge!

CAN YOU HIT THE GOLDEN NOTE?

🎵 **Q1:** Which song was released as a single in 2023?

🎵 **Q2:** At which ceremony was Taylor named Artist Of The Decade?

🎵 **Q3:** Which five producers are named?

Grab a notepad and pen and see how well you know Taylor.
Answers on p122

Album: Lover

just six highlights. There's a lot of well-crafted songwriting here, in line with Taylor's maturing into her third decade of life: "I want to be defined by the things that I love – not the things I hate," she opines in the final track, 'Daylight'.

This time out, Taylor threw herself into press duties with none of the restraint that she'd exercised with *Reputation*, talking frankly about her evolution as a person in interviews with *Entertainment Weekly*, *The Guardian*, *Vogue* and *Rolling Stone*. As she'd done with her previous two albums, she hosted private listening parties with fans in London, Nashville and Los Angeles, and she sparkled in conversation on *CBS Sunday Morning*, *Good Morning America*, *The Ellen DeGeneres Show* and *The Tonight Show Starring Jimmy Fallon*. The media couldn't wait to shower her with appreciation: at the 2019 American Music Awards, Taylor was honoured as the Artist Of The Decade, no less.

Commercially, *Lover* was yet another massive triumph. Taylor's sixth US chart-topper, the album ensured that she became the first female artist to have six albums surpass 500,000 copies sold in one week. In that first week, *Lover* sold more copies on the Top 200 than all the other 199 albums combined. By October 2022, it had gone triple platinum, selling 1.5 million copies in the US.

The *Lover* album was Taylor's first on her new label, Republic, her 12-year contract with Big Machine having ended acrimoniously, as we'll learn on page 82. The plan was to usher in this new era with another world tour, set to kick off in the summer of 2020 – but a certain virus had other plans for us all, and the show was placed on hold for obvious reasons.

However, the *Lover* album wasn't quite done yet: four years after its release, one of its songs – 'Cruel Summer' – was released as a single. Why so? Because that song had been hugely popular on the *Eras* tour, receiving a boost in popularity that made sense to fuel its release, even so long after the parent album. Who could possibly have seen that one coming?

That's a whole lotta dress: Taylor poses at the Golden Globe Awards in early 2020… not long before the Covid-19 pandemic scuppered her plans for a *Lover* tour.

> ❝ *Lover* sold more copies on the Top 200 than all the other 199 albums combined ❞

Images: Getty Images

69

Furry friends

CATS – BOTH AS PETS AND AT THE MOVIES – EXPLORED

The list of Hollywood's worst-ever films – a long list, as we all know – is divided into two categories: movies you can watch for amusement because they're so bad, and films you can never watch because they're just awful.

Cats, the ill-fated musical film of 2019, is one of the latter. Without boring you with too much detail, it was an adaptation of a popular stage show by Andrew Lloyd Webber that had been running since 1981, in which a gang of actors in cat costumes act out a mystical plot laced with many, many musical numbers. There was nothing wrong with the calibre of the actors for the film adaptation – Dame Judi Dench, Idris Elba, James Corden, Jennifer Hudson, Rebel Wilson, Sir Ian McKellen and a certain T Swift among them – but uncanny-valley characters, endless cringe-inducing song-and-dance routines and the massive plot holes combined to make *Cats* a dreadful experience.

So what was the nature of Taylor's involvement? Well, she played a feline femme fatale called Bombalurina. Fortunately for her,

Taylor's role in the *Cats* film casts her as a femme fatale type called Bombalurina.

Furry friends

A mew-sical partnership: Taylor and one of her feline friends take a stroll in New York in 2014.

ALBUM
Folklore
(2020)

TAYLOR'S FOLKY PANDEMIC ALBUM REVISITED

As we write these words many years after the fact, the COVID-19 pandemic is still *technically* ongoing, but most of us would agree that life is a whole lot easier now than it was in 2020 and 2021 when around half the population of the planet was under lockdown. If you were lucky, you spent that time working or studying from home, watching a lot of TV and chatting remotely with colleagues and friends. You might also have listened to a lot of music, which is where Taylor Swift's excellent albums *Folklore* and *Evermore* came in (we'll talk about *Evermore* in a minute).

On her previous albums, Taylor had covered a lot of ground, musically speaking. She'd given us country, pop, soft rock, banging dance tunes

On stage during the 55th Academy of Country Music Awards at the Grand Ole Opry on 16 September 2020 in Nashville, Tennessee.

Album: Folklore

and flavours of R&B music, but – the occasional piano ballad aside – she'd never gone 'full mellow'. This time, responding to the general atmosphere of anxiety and instability that the pesky coronavirus inflicted on the world, Taylor assembled a beautifully relaxed, introspective set of songs with the *Folklore* album. Beats were kept to a minimum, instrumentation was soothing rather than stimulating, and the focus was on slick vocal melodies and lyrics that dealt with family, lovers and reflection – the perfect soundtrack for those endless isolated days.

As Taylor's planned tour dates in 2020 for the *Lover* album were cancelled in April, and the two albums came out in July and December, the new songs represent fast work on the part of Taylor and the team. Nothing sounds rushed on either album, though: in fact, the vibe on *Folklore* is both unhurried and considered. You'd also never know that the music had been recorded remotely, with Taylor doing the vocals from her LA house and producers Aaron Dessner and Jack Antonoff working in Hudson Valley and New York. The songs to check out were also the singles, 'Cardigan' and 'Exile', the former a Lana Del Ray-style intoned love song and the latter a tearjerker duet on which Bon Iver singer Justin Vernon guested.

The album was launched with very little notice, supplying maximum excitement for the

Taylor pictured in January 2020: the singer had big touring plans for later in the year that were cancelled, though she switched gears quickly and produced two surprise albums.

> ❝ Taylor assembled a beautifully relaxed and introspective set of songs with Folklore ❞

75

Test your Taylor knowledge!
CAN YOU HIT THE GOLDEN NOTE?

♪ **Q1:** Why was Taylor's *Lover* tour cancelled?

♪ **Q2:** Who produced *Folklore*?

♪ **Q3:** What was the title of the Disney+ documentary?

Grab a notepad and pen and see how well you know Taylor.
Answers on p122

Album: Folklore

fanbase, who wasted no time playing it – mostly, as you'd expect, via streaming services, as getting hold of a hard copy wasn't always easy in lockdown land. *Folklore* duly broke the record for the biggest-ever opening day on Spotify for an album by a female act, with the two singles hitting charts worldwide and 'Cardigan' becoming Taylor's sixth single to top the US *Billboard* Hot 100. The album was her seventh number-one in a row and went on to be the biggest-selling album of the year.

It didn't stop there, with *Folklore* scooping Album Of The Year at the 2021 Grammy Awards: which made Taylor the first female artist in history to win that award three times. A documentary, *Folklore: The Long Pond Studio Sessions*, was released on Disney+ on 25 November, which captured the phenomenon neatly. Hopefully, we'll never see albums released in these circumstances again, but in the (hopefully unlikely) event of another pandemic, at least we have proof that good music will always be there to keep us sane.

Laura Sisk, Jack Antonoff, Taylor, Aaron Dessner and Jonathan Low, winners of the Album Of The Year award for *Folklore*, at the Grammys in 2021.

Taylor and her then-partner Joe Alwyn collaborated on *Folklore*, with Alwyn netting writing and producing credits on the album.

ALBUM
Evermore (2020)

DOES THE SURPRISE 2020 EVERMORE ALBUM STAND THE TEST OF TIME AS WELL AS FOLKLORE?

Just five months after releasing *Folklore*, Taylor surprised us once again with the issue of its sister album, *Evermore*. Its role, she explained, was to deal with "endings of all sorts, sizes and shapes", the former album having set up a range of situations that required resolution. Like *Folklore*, the new collection of tracks had been recorded remotely and in secrecy with producers Aaron Dessner and Jack Antonoff, mostly at Long Pond Studio in New York State.

The songs had come about in a less organised and more organic manner this time. 'Closure' and 'Dorothea' had originally been written for the supergroup Big Red Machine, which featured Taylor's regular collaborator Justin Vernon of Bon Iver; another song called 'Willow', which eventually became *Evermore*'s opening track, had begun life as a Dessner-penned instrumental called 'Westerly'. Likewise, Dessner's music for 'Tolerate It' was composed on piano before Taylor added her lyrics and sent it back to him.

The music is, like that of *Folklore*, largely mellow and introspective in feel, with restrained beats and Taylor's delivery contemplative rather than extrovert. See 'No Body No Crime', for example, a laid-back country-pop composition featuring remotely-recorded vocals from Haim, and the excellent 'Marjorie', Taylor's tribute to her grandmother Marjorie Finlay. The song was constructed using a program called the Allovers Generator, which randomises sounds into patterns, and Taylor provided Dessner with some old records of Finlay singing, sampled at the climax – the result being one of the more emotional songs on this album.

Released on 11 December 2020, two days before Taylor's 31st birthday, *Evermore* was

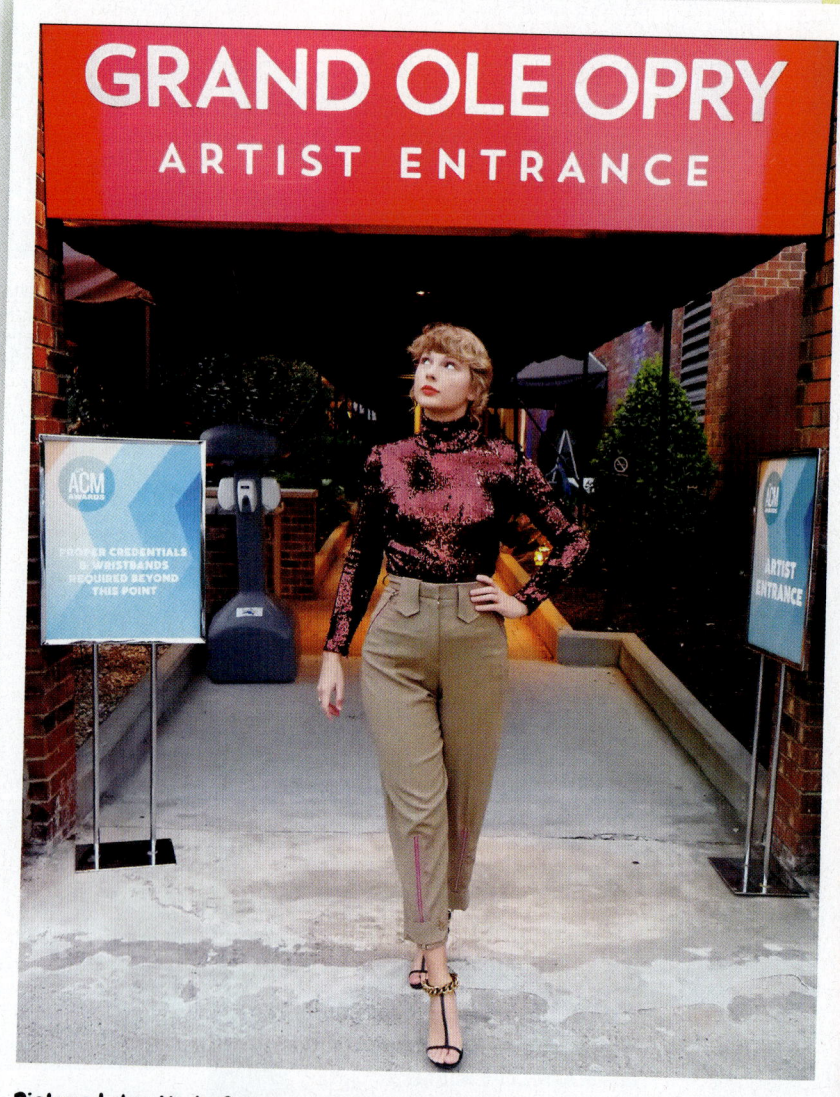

Pictured shortly before surprising us all with the release of Evermore at the end of 2020, Taylor attends the Academy of Country Music Awards at the Grand Ole Opry in Nashville, Tennessee.

Album: Evermore

Accepting the Global Icon Brit Award: no doubt her tireless work ethic during lockdown helped her win the coveted trophy.

promoted under pandemic conditions – in other words, with difficulty. She did appear on *Jimmy Kimmel Live!* in the week of release, but the marketing of the record was largely digital for obvious reasons, with the album released in three separate chunks to streaming media – called 'The Dropped Your Hand While Dancing Chapter', 'The Forever Is The Sweetest Con Chapter', and 'The Ladies Lunching Chapter'. It emerged at the time that Sir Paul McCartney had agreed to push back the release date of his third solo album by a week to avoid a clash with *Evermore* – a decent gesture on the part of the rocking British knight.

Fans were instantly on board with *Evermore*. When the first single, 'Willow', was released alongside the album, it didn't just go to the top of the American charts – it debuted there, the third Swift song to do so. The song was her seventh number-one in the USA, helped by an atmospheric video clip directed by Taylor herself. Two more singles, 'No Body, No Crime' and 'Coney Island', performed similarly on US country radio and US adult album alternative radio respectively, taking the campaign into 2021. The album became Taylor's eighth in a row to top the charts, once again shifting over a million copies in its first week and making her the bestselling female artist of the year.

The question now was for how much longer Taylor would be obliged to stay off the road. Would she release yet more music before the pandemic lifted? All over the globe, Swifties awaited the answer...

Finally getting to perform her *Folklore* and *Evermore* songs at the Grammys in 2021 – that's Jack Antonoff on guitar and Aaron Dessner hiding behind Taylor.

Pandemic-appropriate fashion: Taylor arrives at the 2021 Grammy awards.

Album: Evermore

> "Sir Paul McCartney pushed back the release date of his third solo album by a week to avoid a clash with Evermore"

Test your Taylor knowledge!
CAN YOU HIT THE GOLDEN NOTE?

Q1: Who were Taylor's producers on this album?

Q2: Who was Marjorie Finlay?

Q3: Which types of radio stations are mentioned?

Grab a notepad and pen and see how well you know Taylor.
Answers on p122

Reclaiming her music

HOW TAYLOR CAME TO RE-RECORD HER OLD STUFF... AND CHANGED THE FACE OF THE MUSIC BUSINESS

From the mid-2000s to 2018, Taylor Swift was signed to the Big Machine record label owned by Scott Borchetta, a deal which evidently included a clause awarding ownership of Taylor's masters to the label – the masters being the recordings of her songs, not the actual compositions. When her Big Machine deal expired and Taylor signed with a new company, Republic Records, news came of a dispute between her and her former label over that ownership.

Now, disputes of this nature have been common over the years, but they've never involved a musician whose commercial stature is as vast as Taylor's. A broadly parallel case had involved the metal band Metallica some years previously, with the outcome being that the group purchased their masters from their label for several million dollars. Why would any band do this? Because it permits them to make decisions about the songs' use in commercial licensing opportunities such as TV adverts. This is not just about money, though: it's about artists owning their art.

When the industry executive Scooter Braun purchased Big Machine and its properties in 2019 for a cool $330 million, Taylor wasn't best pleased, labelling Braun an "incessant, manipulative bully" and explaining that she had wanted to buy her masters from Big

The awards keep coming: Taylor Swift with the Best Longform Video award for 'All Too Well (10-minute Taylor's Version)' – more on that in a moment...

Reclaiming her music

That's the look of someone who took on the music industry… and won on her own terms.

83

FAVORITE POP ALBUM

TAYLOR SWIFT
"RED (TAYLOR'S VERSION)"

Taylor in 2006: someone go back in time and tell her not to sign over her masters to Big Machine!

Reclaiming her music

Machine but that the conditions of the deal weren't favourable. She later stated that Big Machine had stopped her from using her songs at the 2019 American Music Awards and in her documentary *Miss Americana*, while also releasing a live album called *Live From Clear Channel Stripped 2008* without her approval.

After Braun sold the masters to Disney's investment arm, Shamrock Holdings, for $405 million, Taylor's solution to the problem was to re-record and re-release those albums – so far: *Fearless*, *Speak Now*, *Red* and *1989* – as she would then own the new masters. Subtitled 'Taylor's Version', the re-recording process began in 2021 and is still ongoing, and people widely endorsed the move. *Billboard* called Taylor "the Greatest Pop Star of 2021", while the USA's largest radio network, iHeartRadio, stated it would replace the old songs on its playlists with new Taylor-owned versions.

The conclusions here are threefold. One, even artists of the stature of Taylor Swift have to abide by the terms of contracts that they sign when they're starting out. The re-recording of the albums would have been expensive and time-consuming, and wouldn't have been necessary were she able to negotiate a deal with Big Machine around 2005 that didn't involve masters ownership. Two, we need to ask ourselves about the nature of music: does it matter if we're listening to an old or new version of a song that we love, as long as they sound similar? It's clear from each re-recording's success that fans are standing with Taylor.

And three: Taylor Swift has redrawn the battle lines of the music industry with the above saga. Masters ownership is now an issue that artists are keenly aware of, and the issue will be doubly important in negotiations to come. Will record deals be as readily available to musicians who refuse to let go of their masters? Maybe, maybe not. Either way, those musicians know more clearly now what their rights are in this area, and that can only be a good thing.

Vindication! Taylor accepts the Favorite Pop Album award for *Red (Taylor's Version)* during the 2022 American Music Awards on 20 November 2022.

Test your Taylor knowledge!
CAN YOU HIT THE GOLDEN NOTE?

Q1: Who bought Big Machine Records?

Q2: Which albums did Taylor re-record so far?

Q3: What is Shamrock Holdings?

Grab a notepad and pen and see how well you know Taylor.
Answers on p122

The silver screen

MEET THE DIRECTOR, MS SWIFT – WHOSE FORAY INTO FILMMAKING HAS BEEN HIGHLY ACCLAIMED

Having sung, performed, written songs and acted on the silver screen, Taylor Swift took a step into a new area of creativity in 2021 by directing her first movie, a short titled *All Too Well: The Short Film*. Its plot was based on the 2012 song of its title, and it starred Sadie Sink and Dylan O'Brien, who you will know from *Stranger Things* and *Love And Monsters* respectively.

You can see the movie on YouTube, where it has accrued close to 100 million views, but be warned, it's a tear-jerker. Around 15 minutes long, it begins with a quote from the Chilean poet Pablo Neruda and is split into seven brief chapters, each detailing a phase in a couple's doomed relationship. The two lovers travel to upstate New York together, they argue after a dinner party, they make up, and they finally break up before a montage of scenes from their later lives reveals that their love never truly expired.

So what does a director do, and how did Taylor approach the job? She answered both questions in a joint interview with *The Banshees Of Inisherin* director Martin McDonagh for *Variety*: "I think I've directed about ten music videos and now one short. I'm just inching my way along toward taking on more responsibility... I wanted to treat [*All Too Well*] differently than I'd ever treated a music video. I wanted to use

The silver screen

Director Taylor with her actors Dylan O'Brien and Sadie Sink at the premiere of *All Too Well*.

a new director of photography that I'd never used before, Rina Yang. I wanted to shoot it on 35-millimetre [film], and I wrote it with Sadie Sink and Dylan O'Brien in mind."

Crucially, Taylor also wrote the screenplay and dialogue, she explained: "I wrote the manuscript, and I had visual references of the art direction. I put together a PDF of what I wanted to make because I'd never made a short before... It's structured narratively in a way that I felt had to be different from any music video I've made. I wanted people to be in that world with these two characters."

The budding filmmaker pulled it off with ease, with *All Too Well* receiving critical praise for her work, as well as nods to the film's acting and

Taylor accepting the MTV VMA for Video of the Year with Dylan O'Brien.

87

Another big win: Taylor's direction on All Too Well won her an AMA in 2022.

production values. When the film came out in theatres and on YouTube on 12 November 2021, it was listed for an American Music Award, a Grammy Award, a Hollywood Critics Association Award and an Art Directors Guild Award. At the MTV Video Music Awards in 2022, the short won Video Of The Year and Best Direction, making Taylor the first person in those awards' history to win the latter award for a self-directed film.

With this critical and commercial success behind her, it came as no surprise when at the end of 2022, the movie studio Searchlight Pictures announced that Taylor had written the script for a full-length feature film, details to be disclosed in due course. With the deft touch and original concept of *All Too Well* behind her, we're optimistic that the project will do well – but who knows? The world of Hollywood can be even less forgiving than the music industry...

Test your Taylor knowledge!
CAN YOU HIT THE GOLDEN NOTE?

Q1: Who starred in *All Too Well*?

Q2: Who is Martin McDonagh, whom Taylor discussed her film with for *Variety*?

Q3: Which studio is working with Taylor on a full-length movie?

Grab a notepad and pen and see how well you know Taylor.
Answers on p122

The silver screen

Taylor discussing her film and performing the titular song at the Tribeca Film festival.

Blue mood: Taylor in *Midnights*-appropriate attire at the 65th Grammy Awards on 5 February 2023 in Los Angeles.

Album: Midnights

ALBUM
Midnights (2022)

HOW DID TAYLOR'S MOST RECENT ALBUM TAKE OVER THE WORLD? MEET US AT MIDNIGHT...

As Taylor accepted MTV's Video Of The Year award on 28 August 2022, she announced that a brand-new studio album was coming on 21 October that year. Not long afterwards, her website was updated with a clock counting down towards midnight – and the hint, 'Meet me at midnight'. You can probably figure out what her new album was called…

Though Taylor's previous albums had all been massive sellers, *Midnights* has topped them all, outperforming her back catalogue commercially and critically, and changing the face of popular music in doing so.

Described as "the stories of 13 sleepless nights scattered throughout Taylor's life" and inspired by five subjects – self-hatred, revenge fantasies, wondering what might have been, falling in love and falling apart – the new songs were Taylor's most evolved to date.

Gone were the cosy, 'cottagecore' sounds of *Folklore* and *Evermore*. With the withdrawal of pandemic conditions by the second half of 2022, Taylor and her audience were eager to celebrate and to let off steam, and although *Midnights* isn't exactly a laugh-a-minute album, it's full of danceable energy in a way that Swifties hadn't really witnessed since

Taylor waves at graduating students during New York University's commencement ceremony for the class of 2022. Taylor, who received an honorary doctorate of fine arts, was the commencement speaker.

Images: Getty Images

the *1989* or *Lover* days. Written mostly with Jack Antonoff, the songs were written in New York, with Lana Del Ray and Taylor's former romantic partner Joe Alwyn earning a co-write along the way. Check out the disco-pop of 'Lavender Haze', the drones of 'Maroon', the alternative rock of 'You're On Your Own, Kid' and the semi-industrial 'Vigilante Shit' for evidence that wherever Taylor was going, it was away from the comfortable sofa-pop of the lockdown days.

On 21 September 2022, Taylor's team released a series of short videos on TikTok that revealed the titles of the new songs. The album itself was followed by four music videos, directed by Taylor, for the songs 'Anti-Hero', 'Bejeweled', 'Lavender Haze' and a remix of 'Karma', and she appeared on *The Tonight Show Starring Jimmy Fallon* on 24 October and *The Graham Norton Show* on 28 October.

If you're interested in how the album did commercially, allow the following bits of data to blow your mind: *Midnights* became Taylor's most successful album yet, selling over 3 million units in a single week and twice that number in two months; it broke Spotify's records for the most streamed album in a single day and the fastest album to stream 700 million times in a week; all of its tracks entered the *Billboard* Global 200, setting a new record; it stayed at the top of the *Billboard* 200 for six weeks; and it was 2022's bestselling vinyl LP and CD. These statistics don't come close to describing the full impact of *Midnights*, which made a huge splash in dozens of countries around the world in ways that most of us haven't even contemplated.

Oh, and what happened next? On 1 November 2022, Taylor announced the Eras Tour, causing Ticketmaster's servers to crash the moment tickets went on sale a fortnight later. Even so, on that first day, over two million tickets were sold. You could not make this up.

Taylor accepting the 2023 MTV Video Of The Year award for Midnights' lead track, 'Anti-Hero'.

Taylor announced Midnights at the 2022 MTV VMA awards.

Test your Taylor knowledge!
CAN YOU HIT THE GOLDEN NOTE?

Q1: Who got co-writer credits on *Midnights*?

Q2: How many units did the album sell in its first week?

Q3: Which two TV shows are mentioned?

Grab a notepad and pen and see how well you know Taylor.
Answers on p122

Album: Midnights

> "It has become the first concert tour to gross over $1 billion across its two-year run"

Performing at Estadio Olímpico Nilton Santos on 17 November 2023 in Rio de Janeiro, Brazil.

The Eras Tour

INSIDE THE BIGGEST POP SHOWS IN MUSIC HISTORY – THE PLANET-CONQUERING ERAS TOUR

When Taylor announced that she would embark on 27 North American dates from March to August 2023, demand was so great that she added 28 new dates – before expanding the tour's remit to cover South America, Asia, Europe and Australia. Of course, when ten times the expected number of applications were made at Ticketmaster's website, it crashed: fortunately, the company wasn't the only entity handling ticket sales, and the Eras Tour dates promptly sold out.

On 17 March 2023, 70,000 fans gathered to witness the opening night at the State Farm Stadium in Glendale, Arizona. They were rocked by Paramore and Gayle, the supporting acts before Taylor herself came on to kick off the main show. The same venue also hosted the tour's second night on 18 March, prompting Glendale to briefly rename itself Swift City. A reviewer from *The Atlantic* summed up: "The turning of one 'era' to the next was like the turning of a pop-up-book page, revealing new colours, architecture, and storylines... The concert had been unbelievable, but so was the fact that this one human woman planned to do it again the next night, and for many after."

Taylor, dancers and crew attend the *Taylor Swift: The Eras Tour* movie premiere in Los Angeles.

At 44 songs, ten acts – one for each of Taylor's albums – and a mammoth three-and-a-quarter hours, each show is a huge undertaking. By and large, the setlist has been the same for each performance, although opening acts have varied, including Paramore, Haim, Phoebe Bridgers, Gracie Abrams, Sabrina Carpenter and more.

The 'Eras' covered in the show are (deep breath): the *Lover* era (including the songs 'Cruel Summer' and 'The Man'), the *Fearless* era ('You Belong With Me', 'Love Story') *Evermore* ('Willow', 'Marjorie', 'Champagne Problems' and others), *Reputation* ('...Ready For It?', 'Indelicate', 'Don't Blame Me' and a massive 'Look What You Made Me Do'), *Speak Now* (just one song: 'Enchanted'), *Red* ('We Are Never Ever Getting Back Together', '22', 'I Knew You Were Trouble', the ten-minute version of 'All Too Well'), *Folklore* ('August', 'Illicit Affairs', 'My Tears Ricochet', 'Cardigan' and many more), *1989* ('Shake It Off', 'Wildest Dreams', 'Bad Blood' and others), 'Acoustic' (any of over 100 different songs!) and *Midnights* ('Lavender Haze', 'Anti-Hero', 'Midnight Rain', 'Vigilante Shit', 'Bejeweled', 'Mastermind' and finally 'Karma'). Now that's a setlist – and if you can't make it to any of the shows, you can watch the accompanying film *Taylor Swift: The Eras Tour*.

Such is the scale of the Eras Tour that some outlets are calling it a record-breaker, and a game-changer. It has become the first concert tour to gross over $1 billion across its two-year run. There's no doubt about it: Taylor Swift's Eras Tour is the concert tour of the decade, and quite possibly of her generation. No one is likely to outperform Taylor as a live artist in the next few years at least – not The Rolling Stones, not Paul McCartney, not the Foo Fighters, not Drake or Beyoncé, Ariana Grande or The Weeknd. Taylor Swift is now the hottest in-concert performer on earth, with all that the title implies: catch her if you can.

A young fan exchanges friendship bracelets with Taylor at Allianz Parque on in November in Sao Paulo, Brazil.

With several thousand friends at Allegiant Stadium in Las Vegas, Nevada.

The Eras Tour

Test your Taylor knowledge!
CAN YOU HIT THE GOLDEN NOTE?

Q1: How many songs does Taylor play every night?

Q2: Which song does Taylor play from the *Speak Now* album?

Q3: How many songs has Taylor played acoustically on the Eras Tour?

Grab a notepad and pen and see how well you know Taylor.
Answers on p122

Getting personal

WHAT DOES TAYLOR DO WHEN SHE'S OUT OF THE LIMELIGHT?

It's hard to imagine that Taylor ever does anything that isn't work-related, but of course, she is human like the rest of us. So do we know about her downtime?

First off, it is reported by media sources of varying reliability that Taylor has an impressive property portfolio, so she might be resident at one of several locations at any given moment. She bought two adjacent penthouses in New York's Tribeca district in 2014, merging them to make a ten-bedroom duplex, which has been occupied by people such as her friend and *Game Of Thrones* actor Sophie Turner, and family at various times. Taylor bought another, $18-million Tribeca penthouse and a 3,500-square-foot loft in the same building some years later.

Over in Rhode Island, Taylor has a 12,000-square-foot beach house, which is handy for Independence Day parties, and down in Nashville, she owns a condo in Music Row and a large house called Northumberland Estate.

Taylor's former long-term boyfriend Joe Alwyn contributed to the singer's music, having writing credits on *Folklore*, *Evermore* and *Midnights* – however, he used the pen name 'William Bowery'.

Getting personal

When business in California calls, she can be found at a 1934 Beverly Hills mansion of 11,000 square feet, a replacement for a ranch-style home that she sold in 2018 at a profit of $850,000. When she's not working, she likes nothing better than to cook, visit antique stores in search of cool artefacts, or just watch TV with her three cats Meredith Grey, Benjamin Button and Olivia Benson.

But who is Taylor hanging out with when she has downtime? We looked at her squad, but we've yet to explore her romantic partners – even though that subject occupies a vast amount of time for certain sections of the media. We know that her first famous boyfriend was the singer Joe Jonas, way back in 2008: we also know that Jonas dumped her over the phone, an unwise move on his part as Taylor wrote about it in several songs afterwards.

The actor Taylor '*Twilight*' Lautner was next, leading to the relationship being dubbed the tongue-in-cheek title 'Taylor Squared' by the media, but they split and remained friends. The musician John Mayer then dated Taylor (Swift, that is) from 2009 to 2010, with the relationship ending on a sour note, and a brief romance with the actor Jake Gyllenhaal also took place in 2010 – the song 'All Too Well' is based on the

> ❝ No one could have expected Taylor's relationship with the little-known actor Joe Alwyn to last six years ❞

▸ Taylor antique shopping in London. Reportedly, she brought the Portobello Road Market to a standstill, with around 100 people following her every move.

Images: Getty Images

99

> "Taylor has an impressive property portfolio, so she might be resident at one of several locations at any given moment"

A photogenic couple: Taylor Swift and DJ Calvin Harris enjoying a moment together. The pair dated in 2015 to 2016.

Getting personal

courtship. Two years later, Taylor dated Conor Kennedy but that didn't last, either.

The relationship between Taylor and the singer Harry Styles sparked large interest in the makings of a pop power couple. Taylor's subsequent romance with the DJ Calvin Harris was a turbulent one, spanning 2015-16, and appeared to leave an emotional scar on both of them. A relationship with the actor Tom Hiddleston was Taylor's last high-profile liaison, lasting a few intense months in 2016.

No one could have expected Taylor's relationship with the little-known actor Joe Alwyn to last six years, but so it did, from 2017 to 2023, perhaps because both parties worked to keep their personal lives private during that time. They seemed happy together but ended things after their lives diverged. A fling with The 1975 singer Matty Healy then came and went, and today, Taylor is dating American football player Travis Kelce.

While it's hard to deny the temptation to delve into the singer's love life, we must remember she is human and just wants to find love without prying eyes. Let's just leave her alone, shall we?

Taylor is currently seeing Kansas City Chiefs tight end Travis Kelce. The pair regularly attend each other's events.

Test your Taylor knowledge!
CAN YOU HIT THE GOLDEN NOTE?

Q1: How many properties in Nashville does Taylor own?

Q2: What kind of shops does she like to visit?

Q3: Which of Taylor's partners contributed to *Folklore*, *Evermore* and *Midnights*?

Grab a notepad and pen and see how well you know Taylor.
Answers on p122

Images: Getty Images

Giving back

HOW DOES TAYLOR SWIFT SUPPORT HER COMMUNITY AND FANS? BY DIGGING DEEP

Any wealthy person with a soul knows it's crucial to give back to the people who made you rich: there's too much suffering in the world for anything else to make sense. Taylor Swift has been doing this since day one of her success as a musician, taking part in fundraising events and helping to spread the word about urgent causes, as well as making direct donations.

As far back as 2007, Taylor connected with the Tennessee Association of Chiefs of Police on a campaign to protect children online: the following year, she donated $100,000 to the Red Cross to help the victims of flooding in Iowa. In 2009, she performed at the BBC's *Children In Need* event, raising £13,000, and in 2010, she gave $500,000 to assist in the response to floods in Tennessee. In 2011, she performed a benefit concert to help with tornado damage in the American Midwest and gave $25,000 to St Jude Children's Research Hospital in Tennessee.

In 2012, Taylor performed her song 'Ronan', written in memory of a four-year-old boy who had died of neuroblastoma, at the *Stand Up to Cancer* telethon; she also donated $100,000 to the V Foundation for Cancer Research and $50,000 to the Children's Hospital of Philadelphia. In 2016, she gifted $1 million to flood relief in Louisiana efforts, gave $100,000 to the Dolly Parton Fire Fund, and assisted food banks in Houston after Hurricane Harvey a year later. In 2018 and 2021, she donated to the Rape, Abuse & Incest National Network during Sexual Assault Awareness and Prevention

Fellow singer Ali Lohan and Taylor attend the Candies Foundation Event To Prevent Benefit in New York on May 7, 2008.

Giving back

Taylor, Jon Bon Jovi and Prince William perform during the Winter Whites Gala in aid of the homeless charity Centrepoint in 2013 in London, UK.

A Taylor-signed Gibson guitar, valued at $2,000-$3,000, at Julien's Auctions for Musicares in Beverly Hills in 2020.

Yule recognise her: Taylor collects toys for charities on the Plaza on NBC News' *Today* in November 2007.

Month. She also gave $1 million for Tennessee tornado relief in 2020, and again in 2023.

Over the years – and these are only the philanthropic efforts that have been made public, of course; we don't know what private donations she's made – Taylor has also donated items to charities for auction, including books to schools; she has encouraged kids to volunteer in their communities as part of Global Youth Service Day; and she has donated to assist legal efforts and charitable activities by singer-songwriter Kesha and actress Mariska Hargitay.

The Nashville music industry has benefited consistently from Taylor's generosity, with $75,000 going to the city's Hendersonville High School to help rebuild the auditorium, $60,000 donated to the music departments of various colleges, $100,000 gifted to the Nashville Symphony – and a whopping $4 million donated to the building of a new education centre at the Country Music Hall of Fame and Museum.

Taylor has also made donations to individuals, with £23,000 gifted to a London student called Vitoria Mario, $15,500 donated to a struggling mother of six named Lauriann Bartell, and an undisclosed sum going to a cancer sufferer called Trinity Foster, who had hosted a release party for the *Lover* album in hospital. A further $13,000 was gifted to two women named Nikki Cornwell and Shelbie Selewski; $50,000 to the Quarles family, who had lost their father to Covid; and $13,500 for a service dog for Jacob Hill, a boy with autism.

Finally, the ultimate philanthropic gesture came in 2023, when the huge commercial success of the Eras Tour led to bonus payments of $55 million for Taylor's crew. Take note, other billionaires: this is how you do it.

Test your Taylor knowledge!
CAN YOU HIT THE GOLDEN NOTE?

Q1: Which three American states suffered flood disasters?

Q2: Which project received a donation of $4 million?

Q3: How much did Taylor award to her crew in bonus payments in 2023?

Grab a notepad and pen and see how well you know Taylor.
Answers on p122

Giving back

Performing in Nashville, Tennessee: when a Tennessee Senate candidate campaigned on values that would hurt the LGBTQIA+ community, Taylor took a stand.

Standing with us

TAYLOR'S HISTORY AS AN ALLY TO THE LGBTQIA+ COMMUNITY – AND TO US ALL

Taylor Swift is widely known for expressing pro-LBTQIA+ views since 2018, and indeed she's received criticism for not being supportive of minority tolerance before that point… but dig deeper and you'll see evidence of Taylor being an ally since as early as 2011. Her video for the song 'Mean', included on 2010's *Speak Now* album, included a coded scene of a boy wearing a pastel sweater, surrounded by burly jock sportsmen. See also the song 'Welcome To New York', the first track on the *1989* album of 2014, in which she sings "You can want who you want" – and in 2013, she donated to funds for the Stonewall National Monument and presented a Media Award on behalf of GLAAD, the LGBTQIA+ support organisation.

She openly stepped to the plate on the 2018 *Reputation* Tour, dedicating the song 'Dress' to Loie Fuller, a queer 20th-century theatre pioneer. A widespread impact was felt when Taylor posted on Instagram before the US midterm elections, saying of the Republican running for Senate, Marsha Blackburn, that, "She believes businesses have a right to refuse service to gay couples. She also believes they should not have the right to marry. These are not MY Tennessee values." The post also informed young people they needed to register to vote, leading to 65,000 new registrations the following day. If that isn't enough evidence of the power of Swift – and

A rainbow family: Todrick Hall, Taylor and others gather on stage at the 2019 MTV Video Music Awards on 26 August 2019.

Swifties, for that matter – as a political force, none other than then-President Donald Trump commented on Taylor's protest, defending Blackburn with the words, "She's a tremendous woman. I'm sure Taylor Swift doesn't know anything about her," and adding in his usual foot-in-mouth manner, "Let's say I like Taylor's music about 25% less now, OK?"

In April 2019, Taylor put her money where her mouth was, donating $113,000 to the Tennessee Equality Project, an advocating organisation for LGBTQIA+ rights. On 31 May, she began a petition called 'Support The Equality Act' at Change.org, writing a letter including the lines, "Our country's lack of protection for its own citizens ensures that LGBTQ people must live in fear that their lives could be turned upside down by an employer or landlord who is homophobic or transphobic. The fact that, legally, some people are completely at the mercy of the hatred and bigotry of others is disgusting and unacceptable. Let's show our pride by demanding that, on a national level, our laws truly treat all of our citizens equally." The website later reported that over 800,000 signatures had been received; Taylor also wrote to the Republican Senator of Tennessee Lamar Alexander, asking him to vote yes to the act.

In June 2019, Taylor donated a sum to GLAAD and released the pro-tolerance single 'You Need To Calm Down', whose video is said to have inspired a pastor in Colorado to write, "[Taylor is] a sinner in desperate need of a savior… God will cut her down." She also gave an interview to *Vogue* in which she said, "Rights are being stripped from basically everyone who isn't a straight white cisgender male. I didn't realise until recently that I could advocate for a community that I'm not a part of" – a form of apology for being slow to show support, perhaps, but something that can be forgiven.

Taylor presents a Media Award on behalf of GLAAD to the actor Ruby Rose in 2016.

With the actor Jesse Tyler Ferguson and his husband Justin Mikita at Stonewall Inn's Pride celebration in 2019, commemorating the 50th anniversary of the Stonewall Uprising.

Test your Taylor knowledge!
CAN YOU HIT THE GOLDEN NOTE?

♪ **Q1:** Which video shows a boy in a sweater?

♪ **Q2:** Which Senator did Taylor write to?

♪ **Q3:** Which video annoyed a pastor?

Grab a notepad and pen and see how well you know Taylor.
Answers on p122

Standing with us

Swifties posing before attending the Taylor Swift Eras concert movie in Century City, California in October 2023.

110

Meet the fans!

Meet the fans!

WE SAY HI TO THE ULTIMATE FANBASE – THE SWIFTIES

In early history – on 31 August 2005 to be precise – the 15-year-old Taylor Swift created a Myspace account. This platform, which readers under the age of 25 may have heard of but not experienced, was a fairly primitive social media space that allowed musicians to interact with their fans. It was supplanted by the more widely adopted Facebook later that decade, but by then, Taylor had built an online fan community like no other country musician. Her Myspace community eventually totalled 45 million users, sowing the seeds for today's vast, and powerful, network of Swifties.

The key, then and now, to the loyalty and enthusiasm of Taylor's fans is that she personally interacts with them. More than just sending out marketing emails or generic social-media posts – although those exist, of course – she has often been known to contact and support individual Swifties. You might think that an interaction with a single fan might not sell many albums, but consider this: when several million devoted Swifties hear that Taylor has been in touch, on or offline, with one of them, she becomes a friend to them all – a real person who might just click on the message button at any time.

The name 'Swiftie' is thought to have become popular circa 2008: Taylor said in 2012 that

Not just the kids: two generations of Swifties arrive at SoFi Stadium in California in August 2023.

111

she finds the term adorable, trademarking it five years later – and no, that's not greedy; it's a way of ensuring that she can use the word without being sued. Since then, the Swifties have become an integral part of her professional activities: she's sent them gifts, invited them to album playbacks, donated to their causes and even attended their weddings. She's written songs in their honour, such as 'Ronan', about the son of a fan who sadly died aged four; she's commented on their TikTok videos; she's included large numbers of Easter eggs and other secrets in her artwork for them to decipher; and she's inspired thousands of Swifties with the colours and art direction of each new 'era' as it has come along.

In return, the Swifties have stuck by Taylor every step of the way. They supported her re-recordings when they had no obvious benefit in doing so, having already bought the original albums; they watch her TV and film appearances in huge numbers, causing unprecedented viewer spikes; they buy her physical CDs and LPs in support of her battle with streaming services; and they were with her wholeheartedly when she switched from country to pop music, even though various media outlets condemned the move as unwise.

And here's the most remarkable part of all this: the Swifties come from all areas of the population. They're not all young. They're not all left-wing. They're not all interested in fashion. One 2023 survey found that 53% of those consulted identified as Taylor fans, and of those, 44% called themselves full-on Swifties. The sample was split more or less evenly across males and females, and only 55% described themselves as Democrats, less than you might expect given Taylor's views. Most revealingly, 45% were millennials, 23% were baby boomers, 21% came from Generation X, and 11% were Generation Z fans.

Truly, anybody can be a Swiftie. Can you say that about any other artist's fans?

> **"Swifties have stuck by Taylor every step of the way and supported her re-recordings when they had no obvious benefit in doing so"**

Taylor meeting a crowd of Irish Swifties during her Reputation Tour in June 2018.

Swifties arrive to take a free shuttle bus from the renamed 'Taylor Nation Station' in Los Angeles.

Meet the fans!

Test your Taylor knowledge!
CAN YOU HIT THE GOLDEN NOTE?

🎵 **Q1:** When did Taylor set up her Myspace account?

🎵 **Q2:** Which video platform is mentioned?

🎵 **Q3:** What is the quoted percentage of millennial Swifties?

Grab a notepad and pen and see how well you know Taylor.
Answers on p122

Awards and accolades

THE TROPHIES ON TAYLOR'S MANTELPIECE

Winning the CMT Female Video of the Year award – at the 2008 awards ceremony in Nashville.

Awards and accolades

How do you measure success – in numbers or awards? In the case of Taylor Swift, both apply in massive quantities.

Let's have a look at the raw data. Taylor has amassed a personal fortune of over a billion dollars, thanks to over 50 million album sales and 150 million single sales, made up of a mixture of physical and streamed purchases. She has sold tickets worth $1.68 billion to date, according to the live music monitor Pollstar, making her the highest-grossing female touring act of all time. According to Spotify, even though she and they underwent a serious difference of opinion a few years back, Taylor is the only musician to have surpassed more than 250 million streams in one day, and the only female artist to have reached 100 million listeners in a single month. She's also the first woman to record both an album, in this case, *Fearless*, and a song, 'Shake It Off', to certify Diamond (10 million sales), and the only person ever to have five albums sell over a million copies in a week.

Got all that? Furthermore, Taylor's chart statistics are also unprecedented. She has the most entries, and also the most entries at the same time, on the *Billboard* Global 200; she has spent the most time on the *Billboard* Artist 100, with 84 weeks; and she is the solo artist with the

Taylor pictured backstage with her impressive haul at the 2023 MTV VMAs.

Accepting the Video of the Year award for 'Anti-Hero' onstage at the 2023 MTV Video Music Awards in New Jersey.

most cumulative weeks at the top of the *Billboard* 200, with 64 weeks. She is also the female artist with the most *Billboard* 200 number-ones, Hot 100 entries, Top 10 songs, and number-one songs on the *Pop Airplay* and *Digital Songs* charts. That's just the American charts, mind: if we had to list Taylor's worldwide chart stats, we'd fill this entire magazine with numbers.

Those are the figures. What about the awards she's received? Let's just say that her cabinet must be heavily reinforced if she wants to display this lot. She's been the International Federation of the Phonographic Industry's Global Recording Artist of the Year a record three times; she's won 12 Grammy awards – including a record-equalling three for Album of the Year; an Emmy, two Brits, eight Academy of Country Music Awards, 12 Country Music Association Awards, 23 MTV Video Music Awards, 39 Billboard Music Awards, 40 American Music Awards, and – believe it or not – 117 Guinness World Records. You could literally compile a *Guinness Book of Records* devoted solely to Taylor if you wanted to.

Then there's the small matter of honours by the National Music Publishers' Association, the Songwriters Hall of Fame, the Nashville Songwriters Association and the BMI Awards – who named an award after Taylor before giving it to her. *Time* magazine put her on its list of the world's 100 Most Influential People in 2010, 2015 and 2019, and named her Person of the Year in 2023; *Forbes* has included her twice in its 100 Most Powerful Women list; and she received an honorary Doctor of Fine Arts degree from New York University in 2022.

Despite all this, Taylor herself would no doubt define her success as being able to keep her family safe, enjoy her friends' company, exercise her creativity, and enhance the lives of her fans. That's wisdom, right there.

> Better get used to this, Taylor: accepting Breakthrough Video Of The Year at the CMT Awards in 2007.

Awards and accolades

The thrill of getting a Grammy award never fades: here's the evidence in 2010

Test your Taylor knowledge!
CAN YOU HIT THE GOLDEN NOTE?

Q1: Which Taylor album went Diamond?

Q2: How many weeks has she spent at the top of the *Billboard* 200?

Q3: How many Guinness World Records has Taylor won?

Grab a notepad and pen and see how well you know Taylor.
Answers on p122

117

Taylor's legacy

HOW WILL TAYLOR BE REMEMBERED IN YEARS TO COME – IN BUSINESS, IN CULTURE AND IN MUSIC?

Elvis Presley in the 1950s, The Beatles in the 1960s, David Bowie in the 1970s, Madonna in the 1980s, Metallica in the 1990s, Eminem in the 2000s – and Taylor Swift in the 2010s *and* the 2020s. That's how the A-list of commercially biggest, most influential pioneers of popular music runs per decade, and anyone who doesn't understand why Taylor belongs on that list either hasn't seen her sales numbers or is clearly not paying attention.

Unlike any of those musicians, though, there isn't really an obvious artistic ancestor for Taylor. She doesn't look or sound like Madonna, Shania Twain, or Britney Spears, although there's a trace of lineage there if you look hard enough. *Vulture* put this best when they observed: "Swift is an oddball. There is no real historical precedent for her. Her path to stardom has defied the established patterns; she falls between genres, eras, demographics, paradigms, trends."

Taylor hasn't just sold a lot of albums and concert tickets: she's also accelerated cultural change. That will be her legacy, and it's more important than mere sums of cash – so what does it look like?

First off, very few artists in the world of music, other than The Beatles, have executed a complete musical style change more deftly than Taylor Swift, and given that her switch from country to pop to folk and beyond has been so successful, it has opened the door for future artists to do the same. As *Clash Music* accurately remarked: "Without Taylor's breakthrough from country star to pop main girl, genre boundaries would have stayed harsher, leaving no room for walking from hyper-pop to R&B to soul as popstars do now."

Second, Taylor has raised awareness of certain business practices – including masters ownership (the re-recorded albums), streaming revenue (the Spotify dispute) and ticketing (the Ticketmaster law changes) – with a massive impact on the future careers of anyone entering the music business. That's a legacy that can be measured not in freedom, in choices, or in any

You can count Taylor among music legends like Madonna, The Beatles, Bruce Springsteen and more.

Taylor's legacy

The boss herself – untouchable, unsurpassable and impossible to beat, in 2024 and beyond.

The answers

SO, HOW WELL DO YOU KNOW TYLOR SWIFT? FIND OUT HERE!

Early life

| Answer 1 - **BRONZE** (1 point) |
James Taylor
| Answer 2 - **SILVER** (2 points) |
Praying mantises
| Answer 3 - **GOLD** (3 points) |
Alvernia Montessori School

Family ties

| Answer 1 - **BRONZE** (1 point) |
Marjorie Finlay
| Answer 2 - **SILVER** (2 points) |
Merrill Lynch
| Answer 3 - **GOLD** (3 points) |
To give Taylor's demo tape to record companies

Taking some time on the red carpet to hang out with some fans and snap a few selfies.

122

The answers

0–39 points It's you. Hi. You're the problem, it's you.
40–79 points Okay, you're on track but there's still a ways to go.
80–119 points Not bad at all. Taylor would be proud of you.
120–149 points Impressive! We're entering superfan territory.
150–174 points You must be Taylor Swift herself.

Musical inspiration

Answer 1 - **BRONZE** (1 point)
Canada
Answer 2 - **SILVER** (2 points)
The Dixie Chicks
Answer 3 - **GOLD** (3 points)
Eminem and Nicki Minaj

Taylor Swift (2006)

Answer 1 - **BRONZE** (1 point)
Nathan Chapman
Answer 2 - **SILVER** (2 points)
A well-known country musician
Answer 3 - **GOLD** (3 points)
Seven

Fearless (2008)

Answer 1 - **BRONZE** (1 point)
Romeo and Juliet
Answer 2 - **SILVER** (2 points)
Def Leppard
Answer 3 - **GOLD** (3 points)
Twilight

You need to calm down!

Answer 1 - **BRONZE** (1 point)
Playas Gon' Play
Answer 2 - **SILVER** (2 points)
To see Travis Kelce
Answer 3 - **GOLD** (3 points)
Katy Perry

Speak Now (2010)

Answer 1 - **BRONZE** (1 point)
John Mayer
Answer 2 - **SILVER** (2 points)
Six
Answer 3 - **GOLD** (3 points)
110

A proud Andrea Swift supporting her daughter at the 2010 Grammy Awards in Los Angeles, California.

Musical evolution

Answer 1 - BRONZE (1 point)
The Chicks / Dixie Chicks

Answer 2 - SILVER (2 points)
Reputation

Answer 3 - GOLD (3 points)
The Beatles, David Bowie and Madonna

Red (2012)

Answer 1 - BRONZE (1 point)
Ed Sheeran and Gary Lightbody

Answer 2 - SILVER (2 points)
'22', 'I Knew You Were Trouble', 'We Are Never Ever Getting Back Together'

Answer 3 - GOLD (3 points)
'We Are Never Ever Getting Back Together', 'Begin Again', 'Red', 'I Knew You Were Trouble', 'State of Grace', 'Everything Has Changed', 'The Last Time'

1989 (2014)

Answer 1 - BRONZE (1 point)
New York

Answer 2 - SILVER (2 points)
Max Martin, Shellback, Jack Antonoff, Imogen Heap, Nathan Chapman

Answer 3 - GOLD (3 points)
Peter Gabriel and Eurythmics

A sense of style

Answer 1 - BRONZE (1 point)
50%

Answer 2 - SILVER (2 points)
Joseph Cassell Falconer

Answer 3 - GOLD (3 points)
Red lips

Paying homage to her country music roots and rocking out with a banjo.

The answers

Working hand in hand

Answer 1 - BRONZE (1 point)
Thug Story

Answer 2 - SILVER (2 points)
Nils Sjöberg

Answer 3 - GOLD (3 points)
Members of The National and Bon Iver

Reputation (2017)

Answer 1 - BRONZE (1 point)
Kanye West and Kim Kardashian

Answer 2 - SILVER (2 points)
Ed Sheeran

Answer 3 - GOLD (3 points)
British Vogue

Reputation tour

Answer 1 - BRONZE (1 point)
Camila Cabello and Charli XCX

Answer 2 - SILVER (2 points)
'Angels'

Answer 3 - GOLD (3 points)
Netflix

Squad goals

Answer 1 - BRONZE (1 point)
Both were dating a Jonas brother

Answer 2 - SILVER (2 points)
Taylor's high-school friend

Answer 3 - GOLD (3 points)
A prearranged opportunity for paparazzi to take photos of Taylor and her friends in public

Taylor dazzling onlookers in an elegant dress at the 2018 Billboard Music Awards.

Lover (2019)

Answer 1 - **BRONZE** (1 point)
'Cruel Summer'

Answer 2 - **SILVER** (2 points)
The 2019 American Music Awards (AMAs)

Answer 3 - **GOLD** (3 points)
Jack Antonoff, Joel Little, Sounwave, Frank Dukes and Louis Bell

Furry friends

Answer 1 - **BRONZE** (1 point)
1981

Answer 2 - **SILVER** (2 points)
For her cats

Answer 3 - **GOLD** (3 points)
Meredith Gray, Olivia Benson, Benjamin Button

Folklore (2020)

Answer 1 - **BRONZE** (1 point)
The COVID-19 pandemic made live shows impossible

Answer 2 - **SILVER** (2 points)
Aaron Dessner and Jack Antonoff, as well as Taylor herself

Answer 3 - **GOLD** (3 points)
Folklore: The Long Pond Studio Sessions

Evermore (2020)

Answer 1 - **BRONZE** (1 point)
Aaron Dessner and Jack Antonoff

Answer 2 - **SILVER** (2 points)
Taylor's grandmother, an opera singer

Answer 3 - **GOLD** (3 points)
US country radio and US adult album alternative radio

The answers

Doing what she does best on her world-captivating Eras Tour

Reclaiming her music

Answer 1 - BRONZE (1 point)
Scooter Braun

Answer 2 - SILVER (2 points)
Fearless, *Speak Now*, *Red* and *1989*

Answer 3 - GOLD (3 points)
Disney's investment company

The silver screen

Answer 1 - BRONZE (1 point)
Sadie Sink and Dylan O'Brien (and Taylor herself)

Answer 2 - SILVER (2 points)
The director of *The Banshees Of Inisherin*

Answer 3 - GOLD (3 points)
Searchlight Pictures

Midnights (2022)

Answer 1 - BRONZE (1 point)
Jack Antonoff, Lana Del Ray and Joe Alwyn

Answer 2 - SILVER (2 points)
Over three million

Answer 3 - GOLD (3 points)
The Tonight Show Starring Jimmy Fallon and *The Graham Norton Show*

The Eras Tour

Answer 1 - BRONZE (1 point)
44

Answer 2 - SILVER (2 points)
'Enchanted'

Answer 3 - GOLD (3 points)
More than 100

Getting personal

Answer 1 - BRONZE (1 point)
Two

Answer 2 - SILVER (2 points)
Antique shops

Answer 3 - GOLD (3 points)
Joe Alwyn

Giving back

Answer 1 - BRONZE (1 point)
Iowa, Tennessee, Louisiana

Answer 2 - SILVER (2 points)
The building of a new education centre at Nashville's Country Music Hall of Fame and Museum

Answer 3 - GOLD (3 points)
$55 million

Standing with us

Answer 1 - BRONZE (1 point)
'Mean'

Answer 2 - SILVER (2 points)
Lamar Alexander

Answer 3 - GOLD (3 points)
'You Need To Calm Down'

Meet the fans

Answer 1 - BRONZE (1 point)
31/08/2005

Answer 2 - SILVER (2 points)
TikTok

Answer 3 - GOLD (3 points)
45%

Awards

Answer 1 - BRONZE (1 point)
Fearless

Answer 2 - SILVER (2 points)
64 weeks

Answer 3 - GOLD (3 points)
117

Taylor's legacy

Answer 1 - BRONZE (1 point)
Elvis Presley, the Beatles, David Bowie, Madonna, Metallica, Eminem, Taylor Swift

Answer 2 - SILVER (2 points)
"The millennial Bruce Springsteen"

Answer 3 - GOLD (3 points)
Kelsea Ballerini and RaeLynn Woodward

All answers correct as of January 2024

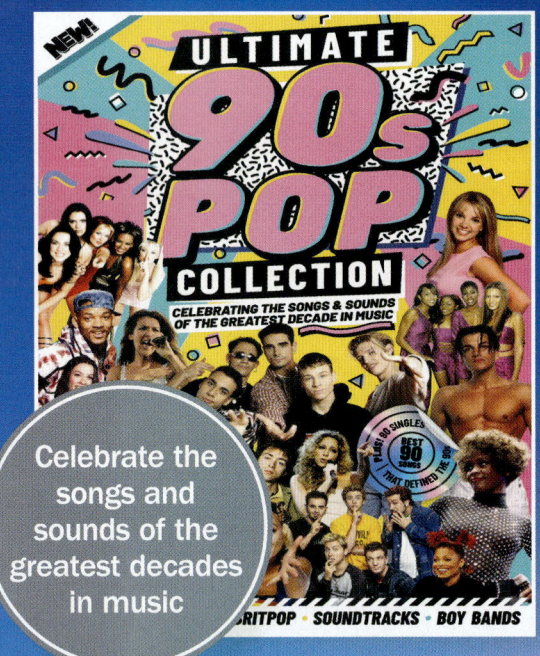

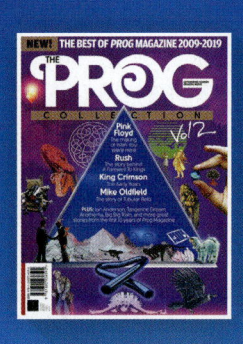

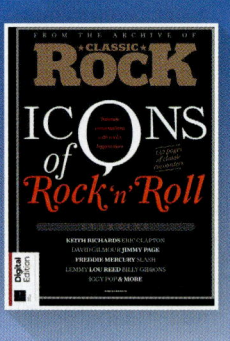

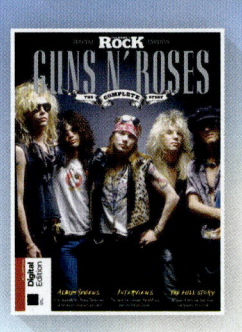

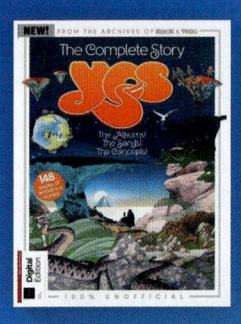

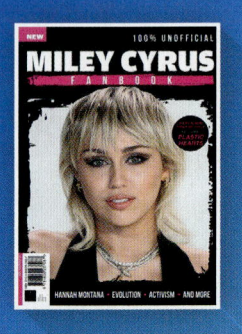

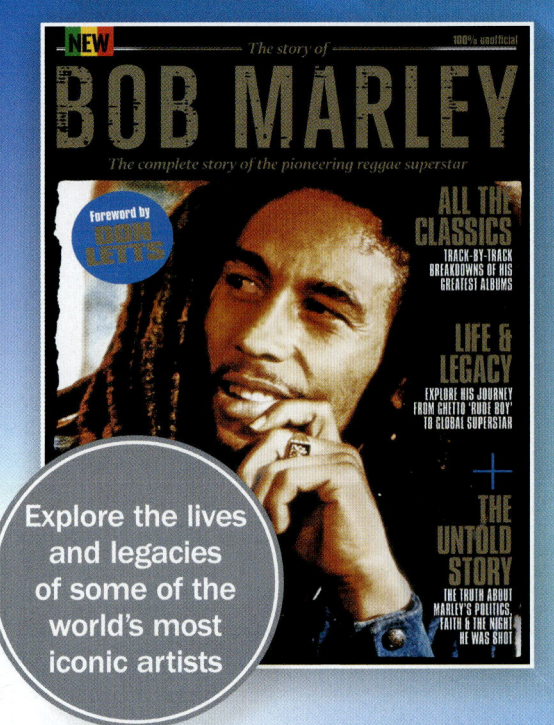

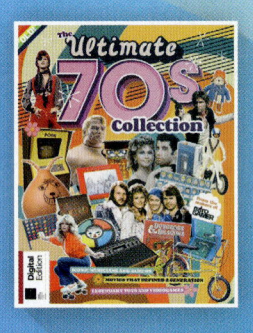

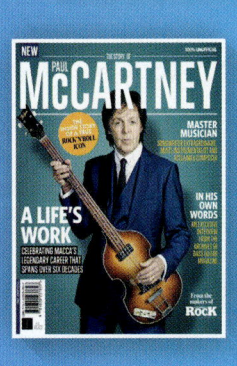

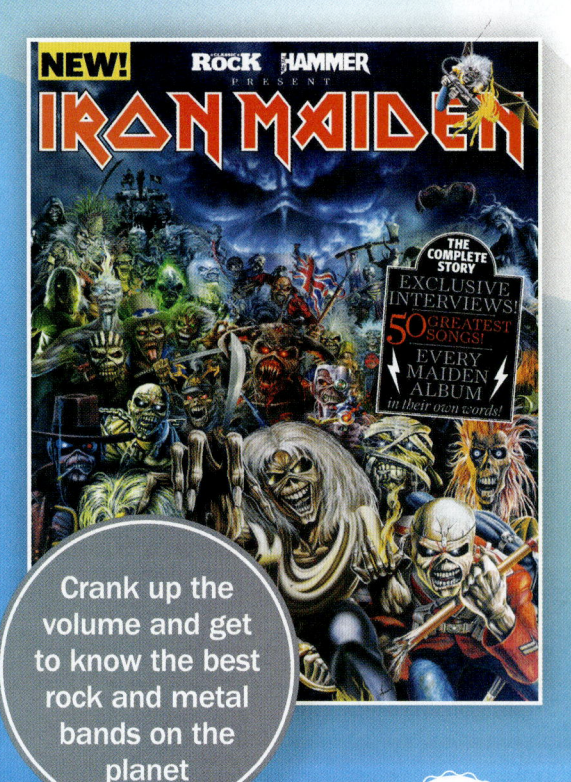

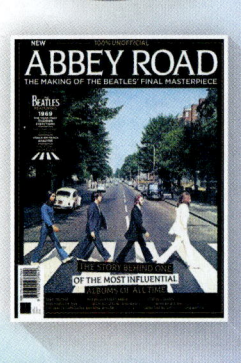

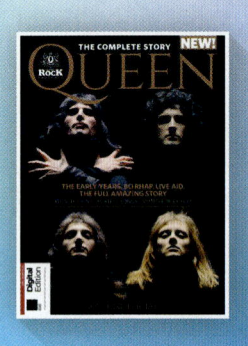

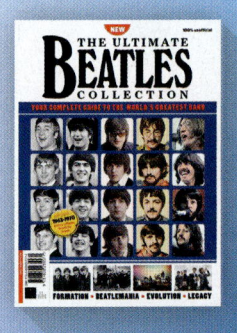

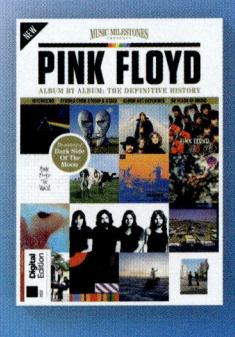

Celebrate the songs and sounds of the greatest decades in music

Explore the lives and legacies of some of the world's most iconic artists

Crank up the volume and get to know the best rock and metal bands on the planet

✓ Get great savings when you buy direct from us

✓ 1000s of great titles, many not available anywhere else

✓ World-wide delivery and super-safe ordering

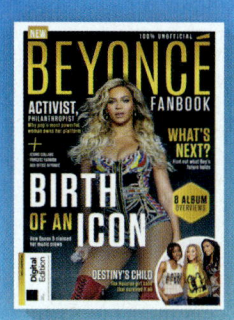

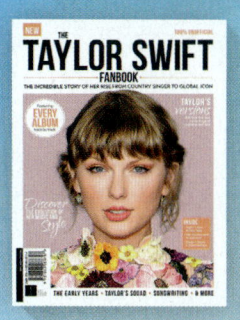

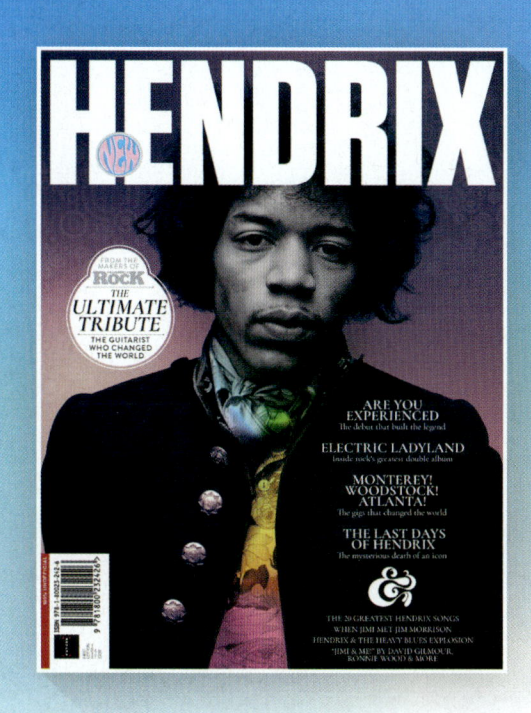

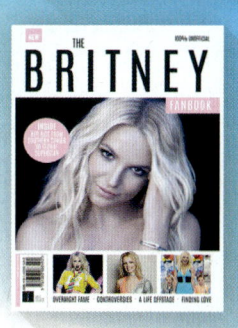

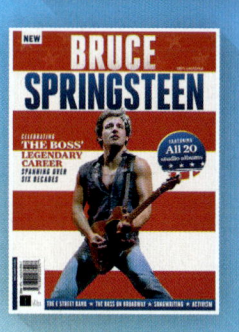

ROCK ON WITH OUR MUSIC BOOKAZINES

Discover the origins of legendary songs, relive iconic performances and meet the pioneers behind some of music's greatest names

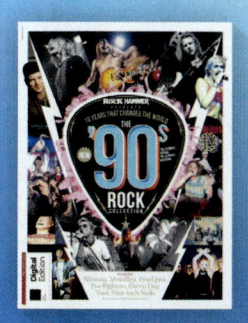

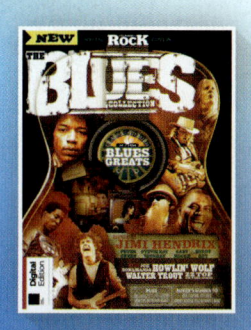

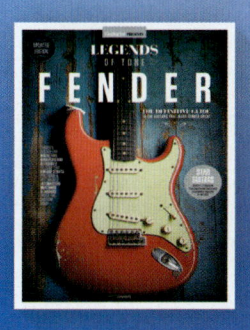

Discover everything there is to know about your favourite pop stars

Follow us on Instagram @futurebookazines

www.magazinesdirect.com
Magazines, back issues & bookazines.

FUTURE

HOW WELL DO YOU KNOW TAYLOR?

Future PLC Quay House, The Ambury, Bath, BA1 1UA

Editorial
Author **Joel McIver**
Editor **Drew Sleep**
Senior Designer **Adam Markiewicz**
Head of Art & Design **Greg Whitaker**
Editorial Director **Jon White**
Managing Director **Grainne McKenna**

Cover images
Getty Images

Photography
All copyrights and trademarks are recognised and respected

Advertising
Media packs are available on request
Commercial Director **Clare Dove**

International
Head of Print Licensing **Rachel Shaw**
licensing@futurenet.com
www.futurecontenthub.com

Circulation
Head of Newstrade **Tim Mathers**

Production
Head of Production **Mark Constance**
Production Project Manager **Matthew Eglinton**
Advertising Production Manager **Joanne Crosby**
Digital Editions Controller **Jason Hudson**
Production Managers **Keely Miller, Nola Cokely, Vivienne Calvert, Fran Twentyman**

Printed in the UK

Distributed by Marketforce, 5 Churchill Place, Canary Wharf, London, E14 5HU
www.marketforce.co.uk – For enquiries, please email:
mfcommunications@futurenet.com

How Well Do You Know Taylor? (MUB5806)
© 2024 Future Publishing Limited

We are committed to only using magazine paper which is derived from responsibly managed, certified forestry and chlorine-free manufacture. The paper in this bookazine was sourced and produced from sustainable managed forests, conforming to strict environmental and socioeconomic standards.

All contents © 2024 Future Publishing Limited or published under licence. All rights reserved. No part of this magazine may be used, stored, transmitted or reproduced in any way without the prior written permission of the publisher. Future Publishing Limited (company number 2008885) is registered in England and Wales. Registered office: Quay House, The Ambury, Bath BA1 1UA. All information contained in this publication is for information only and is, as far as we are aware, correct at the time of going to press. Future cannot accept any responsibility for errors or inaccuracies in such information. You are advised to contact manufacturers and retailers directly with regard to the price of products/services referred to in this publication. Apps and websites mentioned in this publication are not under our control. We are not responsible for their contents or any other changes or updates to them. This magazine is fully independent and not affiliated in any way with the companies mentioned herein.

FUTURE Connectors. Creators. Experience Makers.

Future plc is a public company quoted on the London Stock Exchange (symbol: FUTR)
www.futureplc.com

Chief Executive Officer **Jon Steinberg**
Non-Executive Chairman **Richard Huntingford**
Chief Financial and Strategy Officer **Penny Ladkin-Brand**

Tel +44 (0)1225 442 244

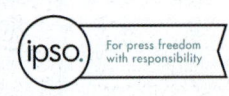